Show Up More

4 Weeks To Freedom, Joy, And The Life You Desire

Jim Sabellico

First Edition published by No Half Cakes 2025

Copyright © 2025 by Jim Sabellico

All rights reserved. No part of this publication may be reproduced, stored or transmitted in any form or by any means, electronic, mechanical, photocopying, recording, scanning, or otherwise without written permission from the publisher. It is illegal to copy this book, post it to a website, or distribute it by any other means without permission.

Jim Sabellico asserts the moral right to be identified as the author of this work.

First Edition

979-8-99889-382-7

ONE

It's Time To Show Up More

You have incredible capacity.

Look at what you've already built in your life. The joy you've created. The challenges you've overcome. The people who count on you. The impact you're already making.

You have the intelligence to solve complex problems, the drive to achieve meaningful goals, and the resilience to handle whatever life throws at you. When you're operating at your best - when you're fully engaged and authentically yourself - you're a force of nature.

But here's what I know about you: you're not operating at your best everywhere you go.

There are contexts where you shine brilliantly and others where you hold back. There are relationships where you're completely authentic and others where you perform a version of yourself. There are areas of your life where you feel confident and integrated, and others where you feel scattered or disconnected.

What if that wasn't necessary anymore?

What if you could show up with the same power, authenticity, and confidence everywhere you go? What if the person you are at your absolute best became the person you are consistently across all areas of your life?

This isn't about becoming someone different. This is about becoming more fully yourself, everywhere.

***

The Power of Showing Up More

Think about a moment when you felt completely authentic and fully engaged - when you were being exactly who you are, using your natural strengths, and making the kind of impact that energizes you rather than drains you.

Maybe it was leading a team through a challenging project, having a meaningful conversation with someone you care about, solving a problem that others couldn't solve, or simply being present for a moment that mattered.

In that moment, you weren't performing or pretending. You weren't holding back or playing small. You weren't worried about what others thought or trying to be who you thought you should be.

You were just you - fully, authentically, powerfully you.

That person - the one who shows up at your peak moments - is who you really are. And that's who the world needs to see more of.

***

The Integration Opportunity

Right now, you probably show up as that authentic, powerful version of yourself in some contexts but not others. You might be confident and decisive at work but hesitant in personal relationships. You might be fully present with your family but distracted and scattered in professional settings. You might be authentic with close friends but perform a different version of yourself in social or business networking.

This isn't a character flaw - it's a massive opportunity.

You already know how to be authentic, confident, and effective. You've proven you can create meaningful impact and build significant success. You just haven't learned how to access that same authentic power consistently across all areas of your life.

What if you could?

What if the confidence you show in your area of expertise became the confidence you showed everywhere? What if the presence you bring to your most important relationships became the presence you brought to every interaction? What if the values that guide your best decisions became the values that guided all your decisions?

This is what integration looks like - not becoming someone new, but becoming more consistently who you already are at your best.

***

My Half-Cake Moment

I discovered the power of showing up more through a moment I'll never forget. October 29th, 2019, 8:45 PM, standing in my kitchen looking at half of my son's sixth birthday cake.

I had missed his entire party because I was "building success" somewhere else. And as I stood there looking at that half-eaten cake, I realized I'd been coming home to half a cake in every area of my life.

Not because I wasn't capable of full engagement - I'd proven I could be fully present and effective when I chose to be. But because I was fragmenting my energy and attention across too many different versions of myself.

At work, I was the decisive leader who had everything together. At home, I was the distracted parent thinking about the tasks waiting for me. With friends, I was the successful entrepreneur who had it all figured out. In private, I was the person questioning whether any of it was worth it.

That night, I made a commitment that changed everything: I would never come home to half a cake again in any area of my life.

But here's what I discovered - this wasn't about working less or achieving less. This was about showing up more authentically and consistently as myself everywhere I went. And when I did that, everything got better, not worse.

***

The Transformation That's Waiting

Over the months that followed my half-cake moment, I learned to integrate the best parts of who I am across all areas of my life. Instead of being work Jim, family Jim, social Jim, and private Jim, I learned to be just Jim - the same person with the same values and the same authentic energy in every context.

This integration didn't diminish my effectiveness - it amplified it. When you're not spending energy maintaining different personas for different audiences, you have more energy for actually creating impact. When you're not constantly switching between different versions of yourself, you can bring your full capability to everything you do.

Today, I can be fully present with my family because I'm not carrying unfinished work stress. I can be fully engaged at work because I'm not guilty about neglecting my family. I can be authentic in all my relationships because I'm not performing different roles for different people.

Most importantly, I can come home each day knowing I showed up as myself everywhere I went - and that version of myself was enough to handle whatever was required.

***

What This Journey Offers You

This book is your roadmap to that same integration. Over the next 28 days, you'll discover how to access your authentic power consistently across all areas of your life.

You already have everything you need to succeed at this - the intelligence, the capability, the life experience, and the desire to live more authentically. You just need a systematic process to bring it all together.

Week 1 (WHO AM I?): You'll strip away the performances and expectations to rediscover your authentic identity, core values, natural strengths, and genuine energy patterns. You'll remember who you are when you're not trying to be who others expect.

Week 2 (WHAT DO I ACTUALLY WANT?): You'll move beyond just solving problems to create a compelling vision of what your integrated life looks like. You'll design a life where showing up as yourself everywhere creates the success and satisfaction you're seeking.

Week 3 (WHERE AM I NOW?): You'll take an honest but encouraging assessment of your current reality, identify your biggest opportunity for integration, and choose the one focus area that will create the most positive ripple effects across your entire life.

Week 4 (HOW DO I GET THERE?): You'll create a specific action plan with clear milestones, weekly steps, accountability systems, and strategies that will turn your vision into daily reality.

This isn't about becoming perfect or eliminating all challenges from your life. This is about becoming more consistently and powerfully yourself, which naturally makes everything else easier and more satisfying.

***

Why This Approach Works

You might be wondering what makes this different from other personal development approaches you've tried. Here's what sets this apart:

It builds on your existing strengths. Instead of assuming you need to be fixed, this approach recognizes that you already know how to be authentic and effective - you just need to learn how to access that consistently.

It's designed for successful people. Most personal development starts from dysfunction. This process starts from capability and helps you optimize what's already working while addressing what isn't.

It focuses on integration, not addition. Rather than trying to add more activities or goals to your already full life, this approach helps you align what you're already doing with who you really are.

It's realistic about your constraints. You don't have unlimited time or energy to dedicate to transformation. This process works within your actual life, not some idealized version of your schedule.

It creates lasting systems. By the end of 28 days, you'll have sustainable practices and frameworks that continue working long after your initial motivation fades.

***

The Exponential Impact

When you learn to show up more authentically everywhere you go, the impact compounds in ways you can't predict:

Your increased presence will deepen every relationship in your life.

Your alignment between values and actions will dramatically improve your decision-making and reduce internal conflict.

Your authenticity will increase trust and respect in all your professional relationships.

Your integration will create more energy for the things that matter most because you're not wasting energy maintaining different personas.

Your example will give others permission to be more authentic themselves, creating positive ripples in every community you're part of.

**

What This Requires From You

This journey requires investment - not of money, but of honesty, consistency, and courage.

You'll need to spend 20-30 minutes each day engaging with the material and challenges. You'll need to look honestly at patterns that might be comfortable but aren't serving your highest potential. You'll need to stay committed to the process even when old habits feel easier.

Most importantly, you'll need to be willing to show up as yourself even when performing a different version might seem safer or more convenient.

But here's what you'll get in return: the most powerful, sustainable, and satisfying version of success you've ever experienced.

***

Your Moment of Choice

Right now, you're at a moment of choice. You can continue managing the complexity of being different people in different contexts, achieving success while feeling internally fragmented.

Or you can commit to the next 28 days and discover what becomes possible when you show up as your authentic, integrated self everywhere you go.

You have the capability. You have the experience. You have the desire for something more satisfying than scattered success.

The only question is: are you ready to show up more fully as yourself?

***

The Invitation

I'm inviting you to join a growing community of people who refuse to settle for fragmented living. People who believe that authenticity and achievement not only can coexist, but actually amplify each other.

I'm inviting you to spend the next 28 days discovering the power of integration - not by becoming someone different, but by becoming more consistently who you already are at your best.

I'm inviting you to prove to yourself that you can create the kind of success that energizes rather than depletes you, that brings out the best in others rather than requiring you to hide your true self.

Most importantly, I'm inviting you to stop coming home to half a cake in any area of your life and start building something whole, authentic, and deeply satisfying.

You have incredible capacity. You've already proven that.

Now it's time to show up more fully everywhere you go.

Your integrated life is waiting. Let's build it together.

Your journey starts now.

TWO

Day 1: Stop Hiding Behind the Mask

Who are you when nobody's watching?

You know that moment when you're driving home from work and you can finally exhale? When you turn off the radio, stop checking your phone, and just... exist? For maybe ten minutes in your car, you're not performing for anyone. You're not being the confident leader, the devoted parent, the successful professional, or the person who has it all together.

You're just you.

And if you're honest - really honest - that version of you might feel like a stranger.

Most successful people spend so much time being who they think they should be that they've forgotten who they actually are. You've gotten so good at wearing the right mask for every situation that you've lost track of what your actual face looks like underneath.

At work, you're the decisive leader who never shows doubt. At home, you're the provider who never admits exhaustion. With friends, you're the successful one who never reveals struggle. On social media, you're living your best life with perfect lighting and carefully chosen words.

But none of those people are completely real. They're all versions of you - diluted, edited, optimized for the audience you're performing for at that moment.

Here's what I've learned after helping hundreds of successful people break free from this trap: the exhaustion you feel isn't from working too hard. It's from being too many different people. It's from constantly code-switching between versions of yourself instead of just showing up as one authentic person everywhere you go.

***

The Mask Collection

Think about all the masks you wear. You probably have the work mask - confident, in control, never showing uncertainty even when you're completely lost. You've got the parent mask

- patient and wise even when you're screaming inside. The spouse mask - supportive and present even when your mind is elsewhere. The social mask - successful and happy even when you're struggling.

Each mask requires energy to maintain. You have to remember which version of yourself you're supposed to be in each context. You have to suppress parts of your personality that don't fit the current role. You have to perform emotions you don't feel and hide emotions you do feel.

No wonder you're exhausted.

The problem isn't that you're not successful enough. The problem is that your success is fractured across all these different versions of yourself, and none of them feel completely real.

I discovered this the hard way when I came home at 8:45 PM to half a birthday cake on October 29th, 2019. My son's sixth birthday party was over. I'd missed it all because I was too busy being the "successful business owner" who never disappoints clients.

Standing in my kitchen that night, looking at that half-eaten cake, I realized I'd been wearing the work mask for so long that my own family was getting the leftover version of who I really was. My six-year-old son didn't know the real me - he only knew the distracted, exhausted version who showed up after hours of performing for everyone else.

That's when I understood: if I didn't know who I was when nobody was watching, how could I expect anyone else to know the real me?

***

The Real You Is Still There

Here's the good news: underneath all those masks, the real you is still there. You haven't lost yourself - you've just buried yourself under layers of who you think you're supposed to be.

The real you is the person who feels energized by certain activities and drained by others. The real you has opinions, preferences, and values that don't change based on your audience. The real you has strengths that come naturally and weaknesses you don't have to pretend don't exist.

The real you is the person you are in those quiet moments when you're not performing for anyone. The person who has thoughts you've never shared because they don't match your professional image. The person who gets excited about things that might not impress other people. The person who struggles with things you'd never admit in a business meeting.

That person - the real you - is who you need to become everywhere.

***

Why This Matters More Than You Think

You might be thinking, "But I have to wear different masks. You can't act the same way with your kids as you do with your employees." And you're right - appropriate behavior changes with context.

But I'm not talking about behavior. I'm talking about identity.

Your core identity - your values, your authentic personality, your genuine energy - should be consistent everywhere you go. The real you should show up in the boardroom and at the breakfast table. Your fundamental character shouldn't change when your audience changes.

When you're truly integrated, you don't need different masks because you're the same person everywhere. You might communicate differently with different people, but you're not pretending to be someone you're not.

And here's what happens when you start showing up authentically everywhere: people trust you more. Your relationships get deeper. Your energy increases because you're not wasting it on performance. Your decisions get easier because they're all filtered through the same consistent identity.

Most importantly, you stop feeling like a fraud. You stop wondering if people would still respect you if they knew the "real" you. Because the real you is who they're already seeing.

***

Your Daily Challenge: The Alone Audit

Today, I want you to spend 15 minutes completely alone. No phone, no TV, no distractions. Just you and your thoughts.

Ask yourself these questions and write down whatever comes up - don't edit, don't make it sound good, just be honest:

1. When was the last time I felt completely like myself?

2. What do I think about when nobody else is around?

3. What parts of my personality do I hide from different people?

4. If I could be completely honest with everyone in my life, what would I say?

5. What do I love that I don't talk about because it doesn't fit my image?

6. What struggles do I have that I've never admitted to anyone?

Don't worry about having perfect answers. This isn't about fixing anything yet - it's about remembering who you actually are underneath all the performance.

The goal isn't to judge what you discover or immediately change everything. The goal is simply to reconnect with the person you are when nobody's watching.

Because that person - the real you - is who the world needs to see more of.

Tomorrow, we'll dig deeper into the values and principles that should guide every decision you make. But for today, just focus on remembering who you really are.

The masks have served their purpose. It's time to show your real face to the world.

THREE

Day 2: The Non Negotiables

The non-negotiables that should guide every decision

Your phone buzzes with a text from your biggest client. Emergency meeting. Today. Right now. The kind of "urgent" request that feels like your career depends on saying yes immediately.

The problem? You already have plans. Important ones. The kind of commitment that matters to the people who matter most to you.

So what do you do? Drop everything and rush to handle someone else's crisis? Or disappoint a client who represents a significant chunk of your income?

Most successful people agonize over decisions like this. They weigh pros and cons, calculate risks, and usually end up choosing whoever screams loudest or pays most. Then they spend the rest of the day feeling guilty about whatever they sacrificed.

But what if I told you there's a way to make these impossible decisions easy? What if you could know instantly - without guilt, without second-guessing, without that sick feeling in your stomach - exactly what the right choice is?

That's what core values do. They're not just nice words on a poster or something you talk about in performance reviews. They're your non-negotiables. The principles that make hard decisions simple because they eliminate options that don't align with who you actually are.

***

When Everything Feels Urgent

Here's the truth about successful people: everything feels urgent to you. Every client request, every business problem, every opportunity that might slip away if you don't act immediately. You've trained yourself to respond to urgency because that's how you got successful in the first place.

But urgency and importance aren't the same thing. And without clear values to guide you, you'll choose urgency every single time - even when it costs you the things that matter most.

Yesterday we talked about how I screwed this up, choosing work over showing up for my family.

Life gave me a second chance to get it right. Or wrong.

The day of hiselevnth birthday, as I'm standing outside the school waiting to pick him up, I got a call that our restaurant's fish tank was leaking. Water everywhere. Seemed like an emergency that demanded my immediate attention. The kind of thing that can't just "wait till later". In the moment it honestly felt like a joke.

Of all the possible days and times for that to happen it had to happen on his birthday. A benchmark moment I screwed up in the past is having to be tested again.

But this time, something was different. This time, I had a clear set of core values that acted like a compass in that moment of chaos.

The question wasn't "How urgent is this fish tank situation?" The question was "Will I miss my son's birthday?" And the answer to that was a 10,000% no. No wiggle room. No negotiation. No exceptions.

Once I knew that answer was absolute, the solution became obvious. I made a phone call to a friend, had them put in a temporary fix, and dealt with the situation permanently the next morning. My son got his full birthday celebration, and the business survived just fine.

That's what core values do - they make impossible decisions simple by eliminating options that violate your non-negotiables.

***

Your Values Are Already There

You might think you don't know what your core values are, but that's not true. You already live by them - you just haven't identified them clearly enough to use them intentionally.

Every time you feel angry about something, you're experiencing a values violation. Every time you feel proud of a decision you made, you're seeing your values in action. Every time you feel conflicted about a choice, it's because the option you're considering doesn't align with who you really are.

Your values are the reason certain behaviors feel wrong to you even when they're perfectly acceptable to other people. They're why you get energized by some activities and drained by others. They're the invisible force behind every decision that felt completely right and every decision you immediately regretted.

The problem isn't that you don't have values. The problem is that you haven't made them explicit enough to use them as decision-making tools.

***

The Difference Between Aspirational and Actual

Most people, when they think about values, list things they wish they cared about or things that sound impressive. They say things like "integrity, excellence, innovation" because those are good values to have.

But those aren't necessarily your values. Those might be aspirational values - things you think you should care about - but not the actual principles that drive your decisions when nobody's watching.

Your real core values are the things you'd defend even when it costs you something. They're the principles you can't violate without feeling sick about it later. They're not just important to you - they're part of who you are.

For example, you might say "family" is a core value, but if you consistently choose work over family when they conflict, then work is actually the higher value in your decision-making hierarchy. That's not necessarily wrong - but it's important to be honest about what your actual values are, not just what you wish they were.

The goal isn't to judge your current values or immediately change them. The goal is to identify them clearly so you can use them intentionally.

***

How to Find Your Real Values

Your core values reveal themselves in three places:

Your anger: What makes you genuinely upset? Not just annoyed, but truly angry? The things that violate your sense of right and wrong are pointing to your core values.

Your pride: What decisions or actions make you feel genuinely proud of yourself? Not proud because other people were impressed, but proud because you lived up to your own standards? Those moments reveal what you truly care about.

Your regret: What decisions do you wish you could undo? Not because they had bad outcomes, but because they felt wrong the moment you made them? Your regret often points to values you violated.

When I missed my son's sixth birthday, I wasn't just sad about missing the party. I was angry at myself because I'd violated a core value I didn't even realize I had: being present for the moments that matter to my family.

When I chose to stay for his eleventh birthday despite the business emergency, I felt proud - not because I was a hero, but because I'd honored what was actually important to me.

Your values are already guiding your emotions. Today's challenge is about making them conscious so they can guide your decisions.

**

Your Daily Challenge: The Values Archaeology Dig

Today, you're going to dig into your own experience to uncover the values that are already there. Set aside 20 minutes and work through these questions:

Anger Audit:

- What are three things that happened in the last year that made you genuinely angry or frustrated?

- What principle or belief was being violated in each situation?

- What does this tell you about what you actually value?

Pride Inventory:

- Think of three decisions you made that you felt genuinely proud of - not because of the outcome, but because of the choice itself.

- What value or principle were you honoring in each decision?

- What pattern do you see?

Regret Review:

- What are three decisions from the last few years that you wish you could undo?

- Not because they turned out badly, but because they felt wrong when you made them.

- What value did you compromise in each situation?

The Compass Test:

- Based on what you've discovered, write down 3-5 core values that seem to drive your strongest emotional responses.

- For each value, complete this sentence: "I will not _____ even if it costs me _____."

Example: "I will not miss my children's important moments even if it costs me business opportunities."

The goal isn't to create the perfect list or impress anyone with your values. The goal is to identify the principles that are already guiding your life so you can use them more intentionally.

When you're clear on your non-negotiables, difficult decisions become simple. Not easy - but simple. Because you're not choosing between competing priorities. You're just following your compass.

Tomorrow, we'll look at how to align your natural strengths with these values to create sustainable success. But today, focus on discovering the compass that's already inside you.

Your values aren't something you need to develop. They're something you need to uncover.

FOUR

Day 3: Strengths vs. Weaknesses

Playing to your natural abilities

Here's a question that might make you uncomfortable: What if you stopped trying to fix what's "wrong" with you and started amplifying what's already right?

Most successful people are obsessed with their weaknesses. You've probably spent more time, energy, and money trying to improve the things you're bad at than you've ever invested in the things you're naturally good at. You hire coaches for your weak spots, read books about your problem areas, and constantly work on becoming more "well-rounded."

And it's exhausting. Not just because improvement is hard work, but because you're fighting against your own nature every single day.

I learned this watching my kids figure out who they are. My son Joseph is a natural athlete - give him any sport and he'll figure it out almost immediately. Hand-eye coordination, spatial awareness, competitive instinct - it all comes naturally to him.

My daughter Marielle, being the younger sibling, wanted to be just like her big brother. So we signed her up for the same sports. Lacrosse, soccer, baseball - all the activities where Joseph thrived.

And every single one was a struggle for her. We'd bribe her to go to practice. We had Joseph try to teach her. We hired coaches for extra training. Nothing worked. She was miserable, we were frustrated, and everyone involved felt like failures.

Then she discovered horseback riding.

Instantly, everything clicked. The connection with the horse, the grace required, the patience and intuition - it was like watching someone step into their natural element. Within months, she was excelling at something we'd never even considered for her.

The same pattern showed up in school. Joseph excels at math - numbers and logic just make sense to him. Marielle struggles with math but has an incredible artistic eye. Most conventional wisdom would say "Marielle needs a math tutor to fix her weakness." But what if instead we got her an art tutor to amplify her strength?

What if, instead of trying to make our kids good at everything, we helped them become exceptional at the things that already light them up?

***

The Weakness Obsession

Somewhere along the way, we learned that "well-rounded" was the goal. That being average at everything was better than being exceptional at a few things. That weaknesses needed to be fixed before strengths could be developed.

This is completely backwards.

Your strengths aren't just things you're good at - they're the activities that energize you while you're doing them. They're the tasks that feel like play even when they're work. They're the areas where a little bit of focused effort produces disproportionate results.

Your weaknesses, on the other hand, are energy drains. Even when you get better at them, they still feel like work. They require constant maintenance and attention. And no matter how much you improve, you'll probably never be more than mediocre at them.

Yet most people spend 80% of their development energy trying to bring their weaknesses up to average, and maybe 20% trying to take their strengths from good to great.

What if you flipped that ratio?

***

The Energy Test

Here's how to tell the difference between a strength and a weakness, and it has nothing to do with your current skill level:

Strengths energize you. When you're using your natural abilities, time flies. You get into flow states. You finish feeling more energized than when you started, even if the work was challenging.

Weaknesses drain you. Even when you're successful at tasks that don't align with your strengths, you finish feeling depleted. The work feels like pushing a boulder uphill. You need recovery time afterward.

Think about your current work responsibilities. Which tasks make you feel alive and engaged? Which ones make you want to procrastinate or delegate immediately?

The tasks that energize you are pointing toward your strengths. The tasks that drain you are highlighting areas where you're working against your natural abilities.

***

The Amplification Strategy

Once you know what your strengths actually are, you have a choice: keep trying to be well-rounded, or start being strategic.

Strategic means structuring your life around your strengths and finding ways to minimize or delegate your weaknesses. It means getting really, really good at the things you're naturally wired for instead of trying to be mediocre at everything.

This doesn't mean ignoring your weaknesses completely. Some weaknesses are fatal flaws that will limit your success if you don't address them. But most weaknesses are just areas where you'll never be exceptional - and that's okay.

The goal isn't to be perfect. The goal is to be authentically excellent at the things that matter most.

***

What This Looks Like in Practice

When you start organizing your life around your strengths, everything becomes easier. Not because the work gets simpler, but because you're finally working with your nature instead of against it.

If you're naturally good with people but hate detailed analysis, structure your role to maximize relationship-building and delegate the spreadsheet work. If you're great at seeing big-picture strategy but terrible at day-to-day operations, focus on vision and hire someone who loves managing details.

If you're energized by creative problem-solving but drained by routine maintenance, design systems that handle the routine stuff automatically so you can spend your energy on the challenges that light you up.

This isn't about being lazy or avoiding hard work. It's about being smart with your energy and focusing your effort where it will have the biggest impact.

***

The Permission You've Been Waiting For

You don't have to be good at everything. You don't have to fix every weakness. You don't have to become a completely different person to be successful.

You just have to become really, really good at being yourself.

The world doesn't need another well-rounded person. The world needs people who are exceptional at their unique combination of strengths and passionate about using them to create value.

Your weaknesses are not character flaws that need to be fixed. They're simply areas where other people's strengths can complement yours.

***

Your Daily Challenge: The Energy Audit

Today, you're going to map your strengths and weaknesses based on energy, not just skill level.

Part 1: Energy Tracking For the next week, pay attention to your energy levels throughout the day. After each major task or activity, note:

- Did this energize me or drain me?

- Did time fly or drag?

- Did I feel engaged or distracted?

- Would I choose to do more of this or less?

Part 2: Strength Identification Based on what you already know about yourself, complete these statements:

- I lose track of time when I'm _____
- People always come to me for help with _____
- I get energized when I can _____
- If I could do only three types of work, they would be: _____, _____, _____

Part 3: Weakness Acknowledgment Be honest about what drains you:

- I procrastinate on _____
- I always need help with _____
- I feel exhausted after doing _____
- If I never had to _____ again, I'd be relieved

Part 4: Amplification Planning Pick your top two strengths and answer:

- How could I do more of this in my current role?
- What would it look like to become exceptional at this?

- Who could I delegate my weaknesses to?

- What would change if I spent 80% of my energy amplifying strengths instead of fixing weaknesses?

The goal isn't to immediately restructure your entire life. The goal is to start recognizing the difference between what energizes you and what drains you, so you can begin making strategic choices about where to focus your limited energy.

Stop trying to be well-rounded. Start being authentically excellent.

Tomorrow, we'll explore what gives you energy and what takes it away, but today, focus on giving yourself permission to be really good at being you.

FIVE

Day 4: Givers vs. Takers

What fills you up and what empties you out

You finally got the promotion. The salary increase is significant. The title looks impressive on LinkedIn. Everyone congratulates you on your success.

So why do you dread Monday mornings more than ever?

Here's what nobody talks about when they're giving career advice: not all success is energizing. You can be really good at something, get paid well for it, and still feel like it's slowly killing your soul.

Most people think the solution to feeling drained is better time management. Get more organized. Be more efficient. Work smarter, not harder. But the real problem isn't how you're spending your time - it's what you're spending your energy on.

Energy and time aren't the same thing. You can spend eight hours doing work that energizes you and finish feeling more alive than when you started. Or you can spend two hours on something that drains you and need the rest of the day to recover.

The difference between people who love their lives and people who just survive them isn't what they do - it's how what they do affects their energy.

***

The Energy Paradox

Here's the thing that trips up most successful people: the activities that make you money or advance your career aren't necessarily the ones that give you energy. In fact, they're often the opposite.

You might be incredible at managing difficult clients, but every interaction leaves you feeling depleted. You might excel at detailed financial analysis, but spending hours in spreadsheets makes you want to take a nap. You might be great at running meetings, but you walk out of every one feeling like you need to be alone for an hour.

The world rewards you for these skills, so you keep doing more of them. You get promoted for your ability to handle the difficult stuff. You get paid more for taking on the draining responsibilities that other people avoid.

And slowly, without realizing it, you structure your entire life around activities that empty you out.

Then you wonder why you feel exhausted despite being more successful than ever.

***

The Hidden Cost of Energy Takers

When you consistently do work that drains your energy, the cost isn't just feeling tired. The cost is everything else in your life suffering because you have nothing left to give.

You come home from a day of energy-draining work and you're too depleted to be present with your family. You snap at your kids because your patience has been used up on difficult clients. You zone out during dinner because your mental energy is completely spent.

Your spouse gets the exhausted version of you. Your children get whatever energy is left over after you've given your best to activities that drain you. Your hobbies get abandoned because you need all your free time just to recover from work.

This is why so many successful people feel like they're failing at everything that actually matters. They're spending their best energy on work that depletes them, leaving scraps for everything else.

***

What Energy Givers Actually Look Like

Energy givers aren't necessarily easy activities. They're not about avoiding challenges or only doing fun things. Some of the most energizing work can be incredibly demanding.

The difference is how you feel while you're doing them and how you feel afterward.

Energy-giving activities share certain characteristics:

- Time seems to fly when you're doing them

- You get into flow states where you lose track of everything else

- Even when they're challenging, they feel engaging rather than draining

- You finish feeling more energized than when you started, even if you're tired

- You naturally want to do more of this type of work

- You find yourself thinking about improvements or innovations in this area

Energy-draining activities have the opposite effect:

- Time crawls - you're constantly checking the clock

- You struggle to focus and find yourself procrastinating

- Even when you're successful, it feels like pushing a boulder uphill

- You finish feeling depleted and need recovery time

- You avoid this type of work when possible

- You do the minimum required and move on

The key insight: energy givers and drains are personal. What energizes one person completely depletes another. There's no universal list of "good" and "bad" activities - only activities that work with your natural wiring or against it.

***

The Energy Audit

Most people have never consciously identified what energizes them versus what drains them. They just accept whatever work they're good at and try to manage the exhaustion that follows.

But once you start paying attention to your energy patterns, you begin to see possibilities you never noticed before.

Maybe you discover that you love complex problem-solving but hate routine maintenance. Maybe you realize you're energized by one-on-one conversations but drained by large group presentations. Maybe you find that creative work fills you up while analytical work empties you out.

Or maybe it's the opposite of all those things. The point isn't to find the "right" energy givers - it's to find YOUR energy givers.

***

Designing Around Your Energy

Once you know what energizes you and what drains you, you can start making strategic choices about how to structure your work and life.

This doesn't mean you get to avoid all energy drains - that's not realistic. But it does mean you can be intentional about the ratio. Instead of accidentally filling your days with activities that deplete you, you can design a life that primarily revolves around what energizes you.

You can delegate or minimize the energy drains. You can batch them together so you're not constantly switching between energizing and draining activities. You can schedule recovery time after particularly draining work. You can negotiate to do more of what energizes you within your current role.

Or, if the energy audit reveals that your current life is fundamentally misaligned with what gives you energy, you can start making bigger changes. Not immediately - but strategically, over time.

The goal isn't to only do things that energize you. The goal is to structure your life so that the majority of your energy goes toward activities that fill you up rather than empty you out.

***

Your Daily Challenge: The Energy Detective

Today, you're going to become a detective investigating your own energy patterns. This isn't about judging what you discover - it's about gathering data so you can make better choices.

Part 1: Energy Tracking (Do this for the next 3 days) Set a timer to go off every 2 hours during your waking day. When it goes off, quickly note:

- What activity were you just doing?

- Energy level on a scale of 1-10 (1 = completely drained, 10 = fully energized)

- How engaged did you feel? (1 = watching the clock, 10 = lost track of time)

- If you could do more or less of this activity, what would you choose?

Part 2: Pattern Recognition After 3 days of tracking, look for patterns:

- Which activities consistently rated 7+ for energy and engagement?

- Which activities consistently rated 4 or below?

- What do your energy givers have in common?

- What do your energy drains have in common?

- Are you spending more time on givers or drains?

Part 3: The Reality Check Answer these questions honestly:

- What percentage of your typical day is spent on energy-giving activities?

- What percentage is spent on energy-draining activities?

- If you could restructure your days to include more energy givers and fewer drains, what would that look like?

- What's one energy drain you could delegate, minimize, or eliminate?

- What's one energy giver you could do more of?

Part 4: The High-Stakes Question Think about your current job, role, or primary responsibilities:

- On balance, does your current life energize you or drain you?

- If it's draining you, what would need to change for that to shift?

- What would it cost you to keep operating at your current energy deficit?

- What would it be worth to structure your life around what energizes you?

The goal isn't to make dramatic changes immediately. The goal is to start recognizing the connection between what you do and how you feel, so you can begin making choices that support your energy rather than deplete it.

Your energy is your most valuable resource. It's finite, it's personal, and it determines the quality of everything else in your life.

Stop treating it like it doesn't matter.

Tomorrow, we'll explore when you felt most authentically yourself, but today, focus on understanding what fills you up and what empties you out.

Because if you don't protect your energy, everything else you're trying to build will eventually collapse.

SIX

Day 5: Your Authenticity Archive

When were you most genuinely yourself?

There's a feeling that comes with being completely authentic that most people have experienced but rarely recognize. It's the easiness of existing. The sense that you don't have to try to be anyone - you just are.

You know those moments when conversation flows effortlessly? When you're not thinking about what to say next or how you're coming across? When words just emerge naturally from what's already in your mind and heart? When you're not performing or posturing, just sharing what's true for you?

Day 5: Your Authenticity Archive   51

That's authenticity. And it feels completely different from the exhausting work of being who you think other people want you to be.

I experience this most clearly when I'm speaking publicly or having deep conversations. When I'm aligned with who I really am, I don't have to think about what to say. I'm not crafting responses or trying to sound impressive. I'm just sharing what's already there - my genuine thoughts, experiences, and perspectives. The words flow because they're coming from a place of truth rather than performance.

But that wasn't always the case. For years, every conversation felt like work. I was constantly calculating what version of myself would be most acceptable to whoever I was talking to. I'd filter my thoughts through what I imagined they wanted to hear. I'd suppress parts of my personality that might not fit their expectations.

The difference in energy expenditure was enormous. Authentic conversation energizes me. Performed conversation exhausts me, even when it goes well.

***

The Authenticity Archive

Everyone has moments in their life when they felt completely genuine - times when they weren't trying to be anyone other than exactly who they were. These moments are your authenticity archive, and they're incredibly valuable because they show you what being yourself actually feels like.

Most people don't pay attention to these moments because they feel so natural they seem unremarkable. But they're actually the most important data points you have about who you really are and how you function best.

Your authenticity archive might include:

- Conversations where you completely lost track of time

- Activities where you felt natural and confident without trying

- Situations where you acted on instinct and it felt completely right

- Moments when you said exactly what you were thinking and it landed perfectly

- Times when you felt energized rather than drained by being around others

- Experiences where you felt like "this is exactly where I belong"

The common thread in all these moments is ease. When you're being authentic, existence feels effortless. You're not fighting against yourself or trying to be someone you're not. You're just flowing from your natural state.

***

The Performance Trap

The opposite of authenticity isn't being fake - it's trying too hard to be the right version of yourself for each situation. It's the exhausting work of constant adaptation, where every interaction requires you to calculate and perform.

When you're performing, even successful interactions feel draining because you're spending energy maintaining a version of yourself that isn't quite real. You might get the response you wanted, but it doesn't feel satisfying because it wasn't really you who got that response.

You can usually tell you're performing instead of being authentic when:

- You're thinking about how you're coming across while you're talking

- You're editing your natural responses to be more acceptable

- You feel tired after interactions that went well

- You're constantly adjusting your personality based on your audience

- You worry about whether people would like you if they knew the "real" you

- You feel like you're playing a role rather than just existing

The exhaustion from constant performance is real. It takes enormous energy to be multiple versions of yourself throughout the day, and it leaves very little energy for actually living your life.

***

The Ease Test

Authenticity has a feeling signature that you can learn to recognize. When you're being genuine, things feel easy in a way that's hard to fake.

The conversation flows without you having to think about it. The decisions feel obvious rather than conflicted. The energy moves through you rather than getting stuck. You feel aligned internally instead of fractured across different versions of yourself.

This doesn't mean authentic life is always easy - you can face difficult challenges while still being completely yourself. But there's a difference between the difficulty that comes from external circumstances and the difficulty that comes from fighting against your own nature.

External difficulty while being authentic feels manageable because you're working with your natural strengths and responding from your genuine self. Internal difficulty from being inauthentic feels exhausting because you're constantly swimming upstream against who you really are.

***

What Your Archive Reveals

When you look back at your moments of greatest authenticity, patterns emerge. You start to see the conditions where you naturally thrive, the types of interactions that bring out your best self, and the environments where you feel most at home.

You might discover that you're most authentic in one-on-one conversations rather than groups. Or that you shine when you're teaching others rather than trying to impress them. Or that you feel most genuine when you're solving problems rather than following procedures.

These patterns aren't random - they're pointing toward your natural wiring. They're showing you how you're designed to function when you're not fighting against yourself.

The goal isn't to only exist in these ideal conditions - that's not realistic. The goal is to understand what authenticity feels like for you so you can recognize when you're moving toward it or away from it.

***

Your Daily Challenge: Mining Your Archive

Today, you're going to excavate your own authenticity archive - those moments when you felt most genuinely yourself.

Part 1: Memory Mining Set aside 30 minutes to think back through your life and identify 5-10 moments when you felt completely authentic. For each moment, write down:

- What was happening?

- Who were you with (or were you alone)?

- What did it feel like in your body?

- What made this feel so natural and easy?

- What were you doing or saying that felt completely genuine?

Part 2: Pattern Recognition Look across all your authenticity moments and identify patterns:

- What environments or situations show up repeatedly?

- What types of people or interactions bring out your authentic self?

- What activities or roles make you feel most genuine?

- What conditions allow you to feel that "easiness of existing"?

Part 3: The Contrast Analysis Now think about times when you felt most inauthentic or performative:

- What situations consistently make you feel like you have to perform?

- Who are you around when you feel most like you're wearing a mask?

- What activities require you to be someone you're not?

- What's the difference in how these experiences feel in your body?

Part 4: The Alignment Audit Based on what you've discovered, honestly assess:

- What percentage of your current life allows for authentic expression?

- Where are you spending the most energy on performance rather than authenticity?

- What would need to change for you to experience more of that "easiness of existing"?

- What's one area where you could start being more genuine immediately?

Part 5: The Practice Choose one situation in your current life where you typically perform or wear a mask. For the next week, experiment with being more authentic in that situation:

- What would it look like to respond from your genuine self rather than your performed self?

- What would you say or do differently if you weren't trying to manage others' perceptions?

- How does it feel in your body when you're authentic versus when you're performing?

The goal isn't to suddenly become authentic everywhere all at once. The goal is to remember what authenticity feels like so you can start choosing it more intentionally.

Your authenticity archive is proof that you know how to be genuine - you've done it before. The question isn't whether you can be authentic. The question is whether you'll choose to be.

Tomorrow, we'll work on crafting a clear "I Am" statement that captures your authentic identity, but today, focus on remembering what it feels like when existence is easy because you're just being yourself.

That feeling is your North Star. Everything you're building should move you toward more of it, not away from it.

SEVEN

Day 6: Who Are You Really

Who You The foundation of who you choose to be

Imagine someone describing you at a dinner party. Not your job title, not your accomplishments, not what you do for work - but who you actually are as a person. How would you want them to finish this sentence: "Oh, [your name]? They're..."

Most people have never thought about this intentionally. They let others define them by their roles, their achievements, or their circumstances. But the most integrated people - those who show up the same way everywhere - have a clear sense of their core identity that transcends any single context.

Today, you're going to craft your "I Am" statement. This isn't a mission statement or a goal for who you want to become someday. This is a declaration of who you choose to be right now, based on everything you've discovered about yourself this week.

***

Why Identity Statements Matter

Your "I Am" statement becomes the foundation for every decision you make. When you're clear on who you are at your core, choices become simpler because you can filter them through your identity.

Should you take that job opportunity? Does it allow you to be who you are, or does it require you to become someone you're not?

Should you agree to that commitment? Does it align with your core identity, or does it pull you away from who you really are?

Should you respond to that conflict in a certain way? How would the person described in your "I Am" statement handle this situation?

When you know who you are, you stop making decisions based on what others expect, what looks impressive, or what feels urgent in the moment. You start making decisions based on what aligns with your authentic identity.

My personal "I Am" statement is: "I am a bold and compassionate leader who rejoices in life's valleys, empowering others to find true success and freedom through God's grace."

This statement guides everything I do. When I'm facing a difficult decision, I ask myself: "What would a bold and compassionate leader do? How can I empower others through this choice? How can I rejoice in this challenge rather than just endure it?"

It's not locked in concrete forever - it can evolve as I grow. But having this clear identity helps me show up consistently across all areas of life.

***

The Five Things Process

The best "I Am" statements don't come from thinking abstractly about who you want to be. They come from looking at who you already are when you're at your best.

Here's the process that works: Start with what you naturally love doing, then extract the deeper identity that those activities reveal.

Think about the five things you most enjoy doing. Not things you're supposed to enjoy, not things that make you money, not things that impress other people - the activities that genuinely energize you and make you feel most alive.

These activities are clues to your core identity. They reveal your natural leadership qualities, your core values, and the unique way you impact the world around you.

For example, if you love teaching others, that might reveal that you're naturally a guide or mentor. If you love organizing events, that might show you're a connector who brings people together. If you love solving complex problems, that might indicate you're an innovator who thrives on challenges.

The goal is to look past the activity to the deeper identity it represents.

***

From Activities to Identity

Once you identify your five favorite activities, ask yourself these questions about each one:

- What role do I naturally play when doing this?

- What qualities does this activity bring out in me?

- How do I impact others when I'm engaged in this?

- What values am I expressing through this activity?

- What does this reveal about who I am at my core?

Look for patterns across all five activities. You'll start to see common themes - qualities that show up regardless of the specific context. These are the core elements of your identity.

Some people discover they're natural encouragers who lift others up. Others realize they're strategic thinkers who bring clarity to confusion. Some find they're bridge-builders who connect different types of people. Others see they're protectors who stand up for what's right.

There's no right or wrong identity - only authentic or inauthentic. The goal is to discover who you already are when you're functioning at your best.

***

Crafting Your Statement

Your "I Am" statement should be short, descriptive, and empowering. It should capture both your character (who you are) and your impact (how you show up in the world).

Here are some examples of strong "I Am" statements:

"I am a bold man who acts out of love and service."

"I am a giving and faithful woman who brings calm to people's chaos."

"I am a creative and courageous leader who helps others see new possibilities."

"I am a thoughtful and determined person who creates solutions where others see problems."

Notice that each statement includes:

- Character qualities (bold, giving, creative, thoughtful)

- How they show up (acts out of love, brings calm, helps others see, creates solutions)

- The impact they have on others or the world

Your statement should feel empowering when you read it. It should make you think, "Yes, that's exactly who I am and how I want to be known." It should capture the person you are when you're operating from your authentic self.

***

The Living Document

Your "I Am" statement isn't meant to be perfect or permanent. It's a living document that can evolve as you grow and change. The goal isn't to lock yourself into a box - it's to give yourself a foundation to build from.

Some people refine their statement multiple times before it feels right. Others find their first draft captures exactly who they are. Both approaches are fine.

What matters is that your statement feels true to who you are right now and empowering for who you're becoming.

***

Your Daily Challenge: The Identity Declaration

Today, you're going to craft your own "I Am" statement using the process we've outlined.

Step 1: Identify Your Five List the five activities you most genuinely enjoy doing. Not should enjoy, not used to enjoy - what do you actually love doing right now?

Step 2: Extract the Deeper Identity For each activity, answer:

- What role do I play when doing this?

- What qualities does this bring out in me?

- How do I impact others through this activity?

- What values am I expressing?

Step 3: Find the Patterns Look across all five activities and identify:

- What character qualities show up repeatedly?

- How do I consistently impact others?

- What values appear in multiple activities?

- What type of leader or person am I when I'm at my best?

Step 4: Draft Your Statement Using the pattern: "I am a [character qualities] [type of person] who [how you show up/impact others]."

Write 2-3 versions and see which one feels most authentic and empowering.

Step 5: The Joy Test Read each version out loud. Which one makes you feel energized and proud? Which one would you be thrilled to have someone else say about you? That's your statement.

Step 6: The Decision Filter Think about a current decision you're facing. How would the person described in your "I Am" statement approach this choice? Does this help clarify what you should do?

Remember: Your "I Am" statement should feel like coming home to yourself. It should capture who you already are when you're operating from your authentic core.

This isn't about becoming someone new - it's about clearly declaring who you choose to be.

Tomorrow, we'll explore how to live this identity consistently across all areas of your life. But today, focus on getting clear on the foundation: Who are you when you strip away all the roles and expectations and just get down to your authentic core?

Your "I Am" statement is your declaration of authenticity. Make it count.

EIGHT

Day 7: Showing Up

Making your "I Am" statement real

Having a clear "I Am" statement is powerful. Actually living it is where the real work begins.

Most people can articulate who they want to be. They can craft beautiful identity statements that capture their values and aspirations. They can describe their authentic self with clarity and conviction.

But then Monday morning comes, and they're back to being whoever the situation demands. The pressure mounts, the stakes feel high, and suddenly their carefully crafted identity takes a backseat to expedience, fear, or other people's expectations.

The gap between knowing who you are and consistently being who you are is where most people get stuck. And it's the difference between having good intentions and actually living an integrated life.

***

The Identity Test

Your "I Am" statement isn't meant to be a pretty poster on your wall. It's meant to be a living filter for every decision you make and every interaction you have.

The real test isn't whether you can recite your identity statement. The real test is whether you live it when it's inconvenient. When being authentic might cost you something. When staying true to who you are requires you to disappoint someone else or pass up an opportunity.

Anyone can be their authentic self when it's easy. The question is: who are you when it's hard?

If your "I Am" statement says you're a person of integrity, what happens when honesty might hurt your chances of getting what you want?

If you've identified yourself as a bold leader, what happens when boldness might make you unpopular?

If you see yourself as someone who empowers others, what happens when empowering someone else means you get less recognition?

These moments of tension are where your identity either becomes real or reveals itself to be just wishful thinking.

***

The Consistency Challenge

The biggest challenge in living your identity isn't dramatic moral dilemmas. It's the daily choice to be the same person in every context.

It's easy to be compassionate at home and ruthless at work. It's easy to be generous with friends and stingy with strangers. It's easy to be confident in your area of expertise and insecure everywhere else.

But integrated people - those who truly show up more - maintain their core identity regardless of the context. They don't become different people when they change environments.

This doesn't mean you act exactly the same way in every situation. You might communicate differently with your kids than with your clients. You might dress differently for different occasions. You might adjust your approach based on what's appropriate.

But your fundamental character - the person described in your "I Am" statement - remains consistent. Your values don't change. Your core qualities don't disappear. The way you impact others stays aligned with who you've declared yourself to be.

***

The Daily Choice

Living your identity is ultimately about making aligned choices, one decision at a time.

Every interaction is an opportunity to embody your "I Am" statement or to abandon it for something more convenient. Every decision is a chance to reinforce who you are or to drift toward who you think you should be in that moment.

The question you have to ask yourself throughout the day is: "Is this choice aligned with who I've declared myself to be?"

If your identity includes being bold, are you speaking up when it matters, or are you staying quiet to avoid conflict?

If your identity includes being compassionate, are you extending grace to the person who's annoying you, or are you defaulting to judgment?

If your identity includes being a leader who empowers others, are you creating opportunities for others to shine, or are you hoarding the spotlight?

These choices might seem small in the moment, but they compound over time. Each aligned choice strengthens your integrated identity. Each misaligned choice fragments it.

***

When Identity Feels Hard

There will be times when living your identity feels difficult or costly. When being authentic might hurt your reputation, cost you money, or disappoint someone you care about.

In these moments, you have to decide what's more important: short-term comfort or long-term integrity.

Most people choose comfort. They rationalize that this one compromise won't matter. They tell themselves they'll be more authentic next time. They convince themselves that the situation is special and requires them to be someone they're not.

But every time you abandon your identity for convenience, you make it easier to abandon it again. Every time you choose to be someone you're not, you weaken your connection to who you actually are.

The people who successfully live integrated lives have learned to see these difficult moments not as obstacles to their identity, but as opportunities to strengthen it. They understand that authenticity under pressure is where real character is built.

***

The Ripple Effect

When you consistently live your identity, something powerful happens: other people start to trust who you are.

They stop wondering which version of you they're going to get in different situations. They stop trying to figure out what you really think or feel. They know that the person they see in one context is the same person they'll see in every context.

This kind of consistency creates deep trust and respect. People might not always agree with your choices, but they'll respect your integrity. They might not always like your approach, but they'll appreciate your authenticity.

More importantly, you'll start to trust yourself. You'll stop second-guessing your decisions because they'll naturally flow from your clear identity. You'll stop feeling conflicted about how to act because you'll know who you are.

***

The Week 1 Foundation

This week, you've done the foundational work of getting clear on who you actually are:

- You've stripped away the masks and reconnected with your authentic self

- You've identified your core values and non-negotiables

- You've recognized your natural strengths and energy patterns

- You've explored what authenticity feels like when you're operating from your true self

- You've crafted a clear "I Am" statement that captures your core identity

Now the question is: will you live it?

***

Your Daily Challenge: The Identity Commitment

Today, you're going to make a commitment to living your "I Am" statement, and you're going to practice it immediately.

Step 1: The Declaration Write your "I Am" statement at the top of a piece of paper. Read it out loud three times. This is who you are choosing to be.

Step 2: The Commitment Complete this sentence: "I commit to living this identity even when it's _____."

Fill in the blank with whatever makes it difficult for you to be authentic. Examples:

- "...even when it's costly."

- "...even when it's unpopular."

- "...even when it's scary."

- "...even when it's inconvenient."

Step 3: The Test Identification Think about your day ahead. What situations might challenge your commitment to your identity? Where might you be tempted to be someone you're not?

Step 4: The Pre-Decision For each challenging situation you identified, decide in advance how the person described in your "I Am" statement would handle it. Make the choice now, while you're clear on who you are, so you don't have to make it under pressure.

Step 5: The Practice Go live your day with intentional attention to your identity choices. After each significant interaction or decision, ask yourself: "Was that aligned with who I've declared myself to be?"

Step 6: The Evening Review Before bed, honestly assess: Where did you successfully live your identity today? Where did you abandon it? What did you learn about the gap between knowing who you are and being who you are?

The goal isn't perfection. The goal is conscious choice. Every time you choose to live your identity instead of abandoning it for convenience, you strengthen your integrated self.

***

Looking Ahead

Next week, we'll work on clarifying what you actually want to build with this integrated identity. But first, you need to establish the foundation of knowing who you are and committing to being that person consistently.

Your "I Am" statement is only as powerful as your commitment to living it.

The world doesn't need another person who knows who they are but acts like someone else. The world needs people who show up as themselves everywhere they go.

That starts with you. Today. In the next conversation, the next decision, the next choice between convenience and authenticity.

You know who you are. Now go be that person.

NINE

Day 8: The Purge

Getting the negative noise out of your head

Quick question: What do you want?

Not what you should want. Not what would make your parents proud. Not what looks impressive on social media. What do you actually want for your life?

If you're like most people, that question either makes you feel overwhelmed or draws a complete blank. You know you want something different than what you currently have, but when pressed to articulate what that actually is, you stumble.

Here's why: your mind is cluttered with so much noise about what you don't want that there's no room left to think clearly about what you do want.

You don't want to be stressed all the time. You don't want to miss your kids' important moments. You don't want to work with difficult clients. You don't want to feel exhausted every evening. You don't want to worry about money. You don't want to feel like you're failing at everything that matters.

All of that negative noise - all those fears, frustrations, and things you're trying to avoid - creates a constant mental static that makes it nearly impossible to think clearly about what you're actually trying to build.

***

The Problem with Problem-Focused Thinking

Most successful people are excellent problem solvers. You've trained yourself to identify what's wrong and fix it. You see gaps, inefficiencies, and areas that need improvement everywhere you look.

This skill has served you well professionally. But when it comes to creating a vision for your life, problem-focused thinking becomes a liability.

When you're constantly thinking about what you want to avoid, you're moving away from problems instead of toward a vision. And "away from" energy feels completely different than "toward" energy.

Moving away from problems feels reactive, defensive, and exhausting. You're constantly scanning for threats and trying to avoid negative outcomes. Even when you succeed, you only get back to neutral - you don't actually create anything positive.

Moving toward a vision feels proactive, energizing, and purposeful. You're building something you actually want instead of just avoiding things you don't want.

The difference is enormous, but most people never experience "toward" energy because their minds are too cluttered with "away from" noise.

***

The Disguised "Don't Wants"

The tricky thing about negative noise is that it often disguises itself as positive goals. You think you're articulating what you want, but you're actually just describing the absence of what you don't want.

"I want to be less stressed" is really "I don't want to feel overwhelmed."

"I want better work-life balance" is really "I don't want work to consume my personal time."

"I want financial security" is really "I don't want to worry about money."

These aren't visions - they're just problems stated in positive language. They tell you what you're trying to escape, but they don't tell you what you're trying to create.

Real vision is about what you want to build, experience, and become - not just what you want to avoid.

***

The Mental Space Problem

Think of your mind like a computer's hard drive. If 90% of your mental storage is taken up with fears, frustrations, and things you're trying to avoid, you only have 10% left for creative thinking about what you actually want to build.

That's not enough space for genuine vision work.

Most people never clear out the negative clutter, so they never get to experience what it feels like to think from a place of possibility rather than problems. They spend their entire lives in reactive mode, trying to avoid negative outcomes instead of creating positive ones.

But when you systematically clear out all the "don't want" noise, something amazing happens: you create mental space for actual desires to emerge. Suddenly, you can think clearly about what you want to experience, create, and become.

***

The Purge Process

Clearing negative noise isn't about pretending problems don't exist or forcing positive thinking. It's about getting all the "don't wants" out of your head so they stop interfering with your ability to think creatively about what you do want.

The process is simple but requires honesty: write down everything you don't want, then consciously set it aside so you can focus on what you do want.

This isn't about solving all your problems before you can have a vision. It's about acknowledging your problems so they stop dominating your mental space.

Once you name what you're trying to avoid, you can stop carrying it around in your head all the time. You can address the legitimate concerns systematically while freeing up mental energy for creative thinking about your future.

***

The Permission to Want

Many successful people have lost touch with what they actually want because they've spent so much time focused on what they should want or what they're supposed to avoid.

You've been responsible for so long that you've forgotten how to dream. You've been solving other people's problems for so long that you've stopped thinking about what would make you genuinely excited about your own life.

But wanting things isn't selfish or immature. Having desires doesn't make you ungrateful for what you already have. Dreaming about your future doesn't mean you're unhappy with your present.

Actually, the opposite is true: people who have clear vision about what they want tend to be more grateful for what they have because they're not stuck in the mental noise of everything they're trying to avoid.

***

The Energy Shift

When you clear out the "don't want" clutter, you'll notice an immediate shift in your energy. Instead of feeling defensive and reactive, you'll start feeling creative and purposeful.

Problems that seemed overwhelming when they were swirling around in your head become manageable when you write them down and address them systematically.

Fears that felt consuming when they were mixed up with everything else become just one factor to consider when they're clearly identified and separated from your vision work.

Most importantly, you'll create space to reconnect with the part of yourself that actually wants things - not just the part that's trying to avoid problems.

***

Your Daily Challenge: The Complete Purge

Today, you're going to clear out all the negative noise so you can think clearly about what you actually want.

Step 1: The Brain Dump Set a timer for 20 minutes and write down everything you don't want in your life. Don't edit, don't organize, just dump it all onto paper:

- Things you're afraid of

- Situations you want to avoid

- Problems you're tired of dealing with

- Outcomes you're trying to prevent

- Feelings you don't want to experience

- Relationships that drain you

- Work that exhausts you

Write until the timer goes off or until you can't think of anything else.

Step 2: The Category Sort Look at your list and group similar items together:

- Career/work concerns

- Relationship/family issues

- Financial worries

- Health/energy problems

- Time/schedule frustrations

- Personal growth obstacles

Step 3: The Reality Check For each category, ask yourself:

- Which of these are legitimate concerns I need to address?

- Which of these are fears about things that might never happen?

- Which of these are outside my control?

- Which of these am I carrying around unnecessarily?

Step 4: The Conscious Setting Aside For each item on your list, make a conscious decision:

- If it's a legitimate concern, write down when and how you'll address it

- If it's an unnecessary fear, consciously choose to let it go

- If it's outside your control, practice accepting it

Step 5: The Space Check After completing the purge, sit quietly for 5 minutes and notice:

- How does your mind feel now?

- What's the difference in your mental energy?

- What thoughts or desires are starting to emerge in the cleared space?

Step 6: The Commitment Commit to not re-cluttering your mind with this negative noise. When you catch yourself spiraling into "don't want" thinking, remind yourself that you've already acknowledged these concerns and return your attention to what you're trying to create.

The goal isn't to eliminate all problems or never think about challenges again. The goal is to clear mental space so you can think creatively about your future instead of reactively about your fears.

Tomorrow, we'll start building your actual vision. But first, you need to create the mental space for genuine desire to emerge.

Your mind is prime real estate. Stop letting negative noise take up all the space where your dreams should live.

TEN

Day 9: The Perfect Monday

What does your ideal day actually look like?

Think about your last great vacation morning. You woke up naturally, without an alarm screaming at you. You had your coffee slowly, maybe looking out at something beautiful. You felt present, unhurried, connected to the moment. The day stretched ahead of you with possibility, not just obligation.

That feeling - that ease, that presence, that sense of living your life instead of just surviving your schedule - that's not supposed to be reserved for two weeks a year. That's supposed to be how you feel about your actual life.

But somewhere along the way, we accepted that real life means rushing through mornings, dreading Monday, and counting down to the weekend. We decided that the spacious, intentional feeling of vacation is a luxury we can only afford occasionally.

What if that's completely wrong?

What if you could design your regular Monday to have that same sense of ease and intention? Not the laziness of vacation - the presence of it. Not the escape from responsibility - the engagement with what matters.

Most people hate Mondays because Monday represents everything that feels wrong about their life: the rushing, the obligation, the sense that they're living someone else's priorities instead of their own.

But what if Monday morning felt completely different? What if you woke up genuinely excited about the day ahead? What if your first thought wasn't "I have to..." but "I get to..."?

This isn't fantasy thinking. This is vision work. And it starts with a simple question: If you could design your ideal Monday from start to finish - capturing that vacation feeling of presence and intention in your regular life - what would it actually look like?

Not your ideal vacation day. Not some impossible fantasy where you never have to work. Your ideal regular Monday - the kind of day that, if you lived it consistently, would make you feel like you were actually living your life instead of just surviving it.

***

Why Monday Matters

Monday is the perfect day to envision because it represents your regular life. It's not a special occasion or a break from reality - it's the day that sets the tone for your entire week.

If you can design a Monday that excites you, you've essentially designed a life that excites you. If your ideal Monday feels energizing and purposeful, then your vision is grounded in reality rather than escapism.

The goal isn't to create a day with no challenges or responsibilities. The goal is to create a day where the challenges feel meaningful and the responsibilities align with who you are and what you're trying to build.

***

The Whole Day Vision

Most people, when they think about their ideal life, focus on the highlight moments. The big achievements, the special experiences, the peak moments of success or joy.

But life is mostly made up of regular Mondays. How you spend your ordinary days determines the quality of your entire life.

Your ideal Monday should include everything: how you wake up, what you do first, how you approach your work, who you interact with, how you spend your evening, how you end the day. It should feel like a complete picture of integrated living.

***

Starting from Energy, Not Logistics

The mistake most people make when thinking about their ideal day is starting with logistics: what time they need to be where, what meetings they have to attend, what tasks they need to complete.

But logistics are just the structure. What matters is the energy you bring to each part of the day and the energy you get from each activity.

Your ideal Monday should be designed around your natural energy patterns, your core values, and the things that make you feel most alive. The logistics can be figured out later.

Start with these questions:

- How do you want to feel throughout this day?

- What activities would energize you?

- What kind of interactions would make you feel connected and purposeful?

- What would make you go to bed feeling satisfied rather than depleted?

***

The Integration Test

Your ideal Monday is also a test of how well you understand yourself. If you've done the work from Week 1 - if you're clear on your identity, values, strengths, and what energizes you - then your ideal day should reflect all of that.

A person whose core identity is "bold and compassionate leader" should have a Monday that includes opportunities for leadership and compassion. Someone whose strength is creative problem-solving should have a day that includes meaningful challenges. Someone who gets energized by deep conversations should have interactions that go beyond surface-level small talk.

Your ideal Monday shouldn't require you to be someone you're not. It should be the natural expression of who you actually are when you're operating at your best.

***

Beyond Work-Life Balance

Most people design their ideal day by trying to balance work time and personal time, as if these are competing priorities that need to be managed.

But integrated people don't think about balance - they think about alignment. Their work reflects their values and uses their strengths. Their personal time supports their growth and relationships. Everything works together instead of competing.

Your ideal Monday might include 10 hours of work if that work is energizing and meaningful. Or it might include 4 hours of work if that's all that's needed to meet your responsibilities while leaving space for other priorities.

The question isn't how to balance different areas of your life. The question is how to design a day where everything you do contributes to the kind of person you want to be and the kind of life you want to live.

***

The Specificity Challenge

Vague vision creates vague results. "I want to be happier" or "I want better balance" doesn't give you anything concrete to work toward.

Your ideal Monday needs to be specific enough that you could actually live it. What time do you wake up? What's the first thing you do? Who do you talk to and about what? What does your work environment look like? How do you spend your evening?

The more specific you can be, the more useful your vision becomes. Specificity helps you identify what needs to change in your current life to move toward what you actually want.

**

The Reality Bridge

Your ideal Monday doesn't have to be completely achievable right now. If it was, you wouldn't need vision - you'd just need better time management.

But it shouldn't be complete fantasy either. There should be a bridge between where you are now and what you're envisioning. You should be able to see how your current life could evolve toward your ideal life.

If your ideal Monday requires you to have completely different skills, relationships, or circumstances than you currently have, that's not vision - that's escape fantasy.

Good vision is aspirational but achievable. It stretches you beyond your current reality while remaining grounded in who you actually are and what's actually possible.

***

Your Daily Challenge: Design Your Monday

Today, you're going to design your ideal Monday in complete detail. Don't worry about how you'll make it happen - just focus on what it would look like if you could design it perfectly.

Step 1: The Energy Foundation Before thinking about activities, identify how you want to feel throughout your ideal Monday:

- What energy level do you want to maintain?

- What emotions do you want to experience?

- How do you want to feel about yourself at the end of the day?

- What would make this day feel meaningful and satisfying?

Step 2: The Morning Design Design your ideal morning in detail:

- What time do you wake up, and how do you feel when you wake up?
- What's the first thing you do?
- How do you prepare for the day?
- What does your morning routine include?
- How do you transition into work?

Step 3: The Work Vision Design your ideal work experience:

- What kind of work are you doing?
- Where are you doing it?
- Who are you working with?
- What challenges are you solving?
- How are you using your strengths?

- How does this work reflect your values?

Step 4: The Interaction Map Design your ideal interactions:

- Who do you talk to throughout the day?
- What kinds of conversations do you have?
- How do you impact others?
- How do others contribute to your day?
- What relationships are you building or maintaining?

Step 5: The Evening Close Design how you want to end your day:

- How do you transition from work to personal time?
- What do you do in the evening?
- How do you connect with family or friends?
- What helps you feel satisfied with the day?
- How do you prepare for tomorrow?

Step 6: The Integration Check Review your entire ideal Monday and ask:

- Does this day reflect my core identity and values?

- Would living this day consistently make me feel like I'm being authentic?

- What would need to change in my current life to move toward this vision?

- What's one element of this ideal Monday I could implement this week?

Step 7: The Reality Bridge Identify the gap between your current Monday and your ideal Monday:

- What's already close to what you want?

- What would need to change significantly?

- What's completely within your control to change?

- What would require external changes or support?

The goal isn't to immediately transform your life to match this vision. The goal is to get clear on what you're actually trying to create so you can start making choices that move you in that direction.

Your ideal Monday is a preview of your integrated life. It's what becomes possible when you stop just surviving your days and start designing them around who you actually are and what you actually want.

Tomorrow, we'll explore how you want to show up in your most important relationships. But today, focus on creating a clear picture of what your ordinary days could become.

Because if you can design a Monday that excites you, you've designed a life worth living.

ELEVEN

Day 10: Relationship Dynamics

How do you want to show up with the people who matter?

You can have the perfect schedule, the ideal career, and complete clarity about your personal goals, but if your relationships are fractured, nothing else works.

Your relationship dynamics - how you show up with the people who matter most - either support everything else you're trying to build or undermine it completely.

Most successful people focus enormous energy on optimizing their professional relationships while their personal relationships run on autopilot. They're strategic about how they interact with clients, thoughtful about how they manage their team, and intentional about how they network professionally.

But when it comes to their spouse, their kids, their closest friends - the people who matter most - they just wing it. They assume these relationships will take care of themselves while they focus on everything else.

Then they wonder why they feel disconnected from the people they love most, even when they're spending time together.

***

The Relationship Autopilot Problem

When relationships run on autopilot, they default to whatever patterns you've fallen into rather than what you actually want to create.

You become the tired version of yourself with your family because that's who shows up at the end of long days. You become the distracted version of yourself with friends because you're always thinking about work. You become the functional but distant version of yourself with your spouse because you're focused on logistics rather than connection.

These patterns aren't malicious - they're just unconscious. You're not intentionally choosing to be less present or engaged with the people you love. You're just not being intentional about how you want to show up with them.

But unconscious relationship patterns compound over time. The tired, distracted, functional version of yourself becomes who people expect. Eventually, it becomes who you are in those relationships.

***

The Energy Investment Paradox

Here's what's backwards about how most people approach relationships: they give their best energy to people who matter least and their leftover energy to people who matter most.

You're patient, engaged, and fully present with clients who pay you. You're creative, enthusiastic, and solution-focused with colleagues you want to impress. You're diplomatic, thoughtful, and intentional with people you're trying to influence professionally.

Then you come home and give whatever's left to your family. You're impatient with your kids because your patience was used up on difficult clients. You're distant with your spouse because your emotional energy was spent on work relationships. You're distracted with friends because your mental focus was consumed by professional challenges.

The people who love you most get the depleted version of who you are. The people whose opinion matters least get the best version.

This is completely backwards if you actually want to build a life that feels meaningful and connected.

***

The Identity Consistency Test

Remember your "I Am" statement from Day 6? Your relationship dynamics should reflect that identity consistently across all your important relationships.

If you've identified yourself as a compassionate leader, that shouldn't just show up at work. Your children should experience you as someone who leads with compassion. Your spouse should see the leadership qualities you bring to other areas of life.

If your core identity includes being encouraging and supportive, that shouldn't be reserved for your professional relationships. Your friends should experience you as someone who believes in them and helps them grow.

Most people compartmentalize their best qualities, saving them for professional contexts while defaulting to whatever's convenient in personal relationships. But integrated people show up as the same person everywhere - which means their personal relationships get the benefit of their best qualities, not just their leftovers.

***

The Relationship Vision Process

Just like you designed your ideal Monday, you can design your ideal relationship dynamics. For each important relationship in your life, you can get clear on how you want to show up and what kind of connection you want to create.

This isn't about controlling other people or expecting them to change. It's about taking responsibility for your side of every relationship and being intentional about the energy and presence you bring.

The question isn't "How can I get my spouse to be more supportive?" The question is "How can I show up as the kind of partner who creates an environment where support flows naturally?"

The question isn't "How can I get my kids to respect me more?" The question is "How can I show up as the kind of parent who earns respect through consistent, loving leadership?"

The question isn't "How can I get my friends to prioritize our friendship?" The question is "How can I show up as the kind of friend who makes others feel valued and connected?"

***

The Specific Relationship Audit

Different relationships require different approaches, but they should all reflect your core identity and values.

With your spouse or partner: How do you want to show up as a life partner? What kind of emotional presence do you want to bring? How can you support their growth while staying true to who you are?

With your children: How do you want to show up as a parent? What qualities do you want them to associate with you? How can you be both loving and strong, both supportive and challenging?

With your extended family: How do you want to navigate family dynamics? What boundaries do you need to maintain? How can you be loving without compromising your values?

With close friends: How do you want to show up in friendship? What kind of friend do you want to be known as? How can you maintain deep connections while respecting everyone's growth?

With colleagues and professional relationships: How do you want to integrate your personal values into your professional interactions? How can you be authentic without being unprofessional?

***

The Presence Practice

The foundation of all healthy relationship dynamics is presence - your ability to be fully engaged with whoever you're with rather than mentally somewhere else.

Presence isn't about having unlimited time. It's about giving focused attention when you are together. It's about being mentally and emotionally available during the interactions you do have.

Most relationship problems aren't actually about time - they're about attention. People don't need you to be available 24/7. They need to know that when you are together, you're actually there.

Your phone can wait. Your email can wait. Your mental to-do list can wait. The person in front of you - especially if they're someone you love - deserves your focused attention.

***

Your Daily Challenge: Relationship Design

Today, you're going to design how you want to show up in your most important relationships.

Step 1: The Priority List List your 5-7 most important relationships. Include:

- Immediate family members

- Close friends who matter to you

- Professional relationships that are personally significant

- Anyone whose opinion and connection you deeply value

Step 2: The Current State Assessment For each relationship, honestly assess how you currently show up:

- What version of yourself do they typically see?

- What energy do you usually bring to interactions with them?

- How present are you when you're together?

- What do they probably think are your priorities based on how you act?

Step 3: The Identity Integration For each relationship, consider how your core identity should show up:

- If you're a compassionate leader, how should that manifest in this relationship?

- If you're encouraging and supportive, how should they experience that?

- What qualities from your "I Am" statement should be evident to this person?

Step 4: The Ideal Dynamic Design For each relationship, envision how you want to show up:

- What energy do you want to bring to interactions?

- How do you want them to feel when they're with you?

- What kind of connection do you want to create?

- How do you want to contribute to their life and growth?

Step 5: The Specific Changes For each relationship, identify specific changes you can make:

- What would you do differently in your next interaction?

- How could you be more present when you're together?

- What conversations have you been avoiding that would strengthen the connection?

- How could you better reflect your authentic identity in this relationship?

Step 6: The Energy Audit Look at your overall relationship patterns:

- Are you giving your best energy to the relationships that matter most?

- Where are you being intentional vs. running on autopilot?

- What needs to change about how you prioritize your relational energy?

Step 7: The Practice Plan Choose one relationship to focus on this week:

- What specific changes will you make in how you show up?

- How will you be more present and intentional?

- What will you do to bring your authentic identity into this relationship?

The goal isn't to suddenly become perfect in all your relationships. The goal is to start being as intentional about your personal relationships as you are about your professional ones.

Your relationships either support your integrated life or fragment it. When you show up as the same authentic person everywhere, your relationships become sources of energy rather than drains on your energy.

Tomorrow, we'll explore how you want your work to serve your whole life rather than consume it. But today, focus on how you want to show up with the people who matter most.

Because at the end of your life, the quality of your relationships will matter more than any other success you achieve.

TWELVE

Day 11: Work That Works

Designing a career that serves your whole life

Most people have their relationship with work completely backwards.

They think work exists to provide money so they can live their real life on nights and weekends. They accept that Monday through Friday belongs to someone else's priorities, and they try to squeeze their actual life into whatever time remains.

This creates a fundamental split: there's work life and there's real life, and they're constantly competing with each other.

But what if work wasn't something that interrupted your life? What if it was something that enhanced it? What if your career could be designed to serve your whole life instead of consuming it?

This isn't naive idealism. This is what integration actually looks like. When your work aligns with your identity, values, and strengths, it stops feeling like something you have to do and starts feeling like something you get to do.

***

The Work-Life Integration Model

Forget work-life balance. Balance implies that work and life are opposing forces that need to be managed against each other. Integration means they work together.

In an integrated approach, your work reflects your core identity. It uses your natural strengths. It aligns with your values. It contributes to the kind of person you want to become rather than requiring you to be someone you're not.

Your work becomes an expression of who you are rather than a performance you put on to earn money.

This doesn't mean your work has to be your passion or your life's calling. It means your work shouldn't require you to violate your identity or compromise your core values in order to be successful.

***

The Energy Economics of Work

Here's what most people don't understand about work: the issue isn't how many hours you work. The issue is whether those hours energize you or deplete you.

You can work 60 hours a week on something that aligns with your strengths and values and finish feeling energized. Or you can work 30 hours a week on something that goes against your nature and feel completely drained.

The goal isn't to work fewer hours. The goal is to work on things that work with your natural wiring rather than against it.

When your work energizes you, you have more energy for everything else in your life. When your work depletes you, everything else suffers because you're running on empty.

***

The Identity Alignment Test

Your work should be a natural expression of your "I Am" statement, not a contradiction of it.

If you've identified yourself as a compassionate leader, your work should provide opportunities for both leadership and compassion. If you see yourself as a creative problem-solver, your work should involve solving meaningful problems in innovative ways.

This doesn't mean you need to find the perfect job that matches every aspect of your identity. It means the core of what you do should align with the core of who you are.

When there's alignment, work feels natural. You're not pretending to be someone else for 40+ hours a week. You're being yourself in a professional context.

When there's misalignment, work feels like acting. You're constantly performing a role that doesn't fit who you really are, which is exhausting even when you're successful.

***

The Value Integration Challenge

Your core values - the non-negotiables you identified earlier - should be expressible through your work, not violated by it.

If integrity is a core value, your work shouldn't require you to be dishonest or manipulative to succeed. If family is a core value, your work culture shouldn't punish you for prioritizing important family moments.

This doesn't mean your workplace has to share all your values. It means your work shouldn't require you to consistently act against what you believe is right.

Many people accept value violations at work because they think it's just part of being professional. But when you regularly violate your values to succeed professionally, you fragment your identity and deplete your integrity.

**

The Strength Utilization Principle

Remember the energy audit you did earlier? The same principle applies to work: you should be spending most of your time on activities that energize you rather than drain you.

This doesn't mean you'll never do tasks you don't enjoy. But the bulk of your work - the core of what you're responsible for - should align with your natural strengths and energy patterns.

If you're naturally good with people but spend most of your time doing detailed analysis, you're working against your strengths. If you're energized by creative challenges but stuck doing routine maintenance, you're wasting your natural abilities.

The goal is to structure your role (or find a role) where your strengths are assets, not where you're constantly trying to overcome your weaknesses.

***

The Service Connection

Work that truly serves your whole life has a service component - it contributes to something beyond just your personal benefit.

This doesn't mean you have to work for a nonprofit or save the world. It means you can see how your work creates value for others, solves real problems, or contributes to something meaningful.

When you can connect what you do daily to a larger purpose, work stops feeling like just a way to pay bills and starts feeling like a way to make a difference.

This connection between daily tasks and meaningful impact is what separates jobs from careers from callings.

***

The Sustainability Factor

Work that works for your whole life is sustainable long-term. You can imagine doing it (or evolving within it) for years without burning out or losing your sense of self.

Unsustainable work might pay well or look impressive, but it has an expiration date. Either your energy will give out, your values will be so compromised you can't continue, or the disconnect from your authentic self will become unbearable.

Sustainable work aligns with your natural rhythms, respects your other priorities, and allows you to grow as a person rather than just advance as a professional.

***

The Design Process

Designing work that works isn't just about finding a different job. It's about being intentional about how work fits into your integrated life.

Sometimes this means changing careers. Sometimes it means restructuring your current role. Sometimes it means changing how you approach the work you already do.

The key is starting with clarity about what you need from work beyond just money:

- How should it reflect your identity?

- Which of your strengths should it utilize?

- What values must it allow you to express?

- How should it contribute to your overall energy and well-being?

- What impact do you want to have through your work?

***

Your Daily Challenge: Work Integration Design

Today, you're going to design what work that works would look like for your integrated life.

Step 1: Current Work Assessment Honestly evaluate your current work situation:

- What percentage of your work aligns with your strengths?

- How often does your work require you to violate your core values?

- Does your work energize you or deplete you overall?

- How does your current work reflect (or contradict) your "I Am" statement?

- What impact are you having through your work?

Step 2: The Identity Integration Analysis Based on your "I Am" statement, consider:

- What kind of work would be a natural expression of your core identity?

- What roles or responsibilities would allow your authentic self to shine?

- What work environments would support who you really are?

- How could your unique combination of qualities create value professionally?

Step 3: The Strengths Application Think about your natural strengths and energy patterns:

- What type of work energizes you rather than drains you?

- What problems do you naturally love solving?

- What activities make you lose track of time in a good way?

- How could you structure work around what comes naturally to you?

Step 4: The Values Alignment Check Consider your core values:

- What work cultures and practices would honor your non-negotiables?

- What would you need to be true about your work environment?

- What boundaries would you need to maintain?

- How could your work allow you to express what matters most to you?

Step 5: The Service Vision Think about meaningful impact:

- What problems do you care about solving?

- Who do you want to serve through your work?

- What kind of difference do you want to make?

- How could your work contribute to something larger than yourself?

Step 6: The Integration Design Based on everything above, describe your ideal work situation:

- What would you actually be doing day-to-day?

- What kind of people would you work with?

- What would the culture and environment be like?

- How would this work serve your whole life rather than consume it?

- What would need to be true for this work to be sustainable long-term?

Step 7: The Gap Analysis and Action Planning Compare your current work situation to your integrated work vision:

- What's already aligned that you can appreciate and build on?

- What are the biggest gaps between current and ideal?

- What changes could you make within your current role?

- What would need to change about your work situation?

- What's one step you could take this week toward better work integration?

The goal isn't to immediately quit your job and find perfect work. The goal is to get clear on what work that serves your whole life would look like so you can start making strategic choices to move in that direction.

Your work takes up too much of your life to be something that drains your energy and contradicts your identity. When your work aligns with who you are, everything else in your life gets easier because you're not constantly recovering from spending your days being someone you're not.

Tomorrow, we'll explore how you want to show up for your family's most important moments. But today, focus on designing work that enhances your life rather than consuming it.

Because when work works for your whole life, everything else becomes more possible.

THIRTEEN

Day 12: Being Present

Being present for the moments that matter

Your family doesn't need a perfect parent or partner. They need a present one.

But presence isn't just about being physically there. You can be in the same room as your family while being mentally somewhere else entirely. You can attend every dinner, every game, every school event and still be absent from the moments that matter most.

Real presence is about being emotionally and mentally available when you're together. It's about being the same authentic person at home that you are everywhere else. It's about showing up as yourself, not as the tired, distracted, leftover version of yourself.

Most successful people give their best energy to their work and hope their family will be satisfied with whatever remains. But your family deserves better than your leftovers. They deserve to see the engaged, capable, authentic person that everyone else gets to experience.

***

The Family Life Paradox

Here's the paradox most parents and partners face: you work hard to provide for your family, but the harder you work, the less present you become for the people you're working to support.

You miss bedtime stories because you're answering emails. You're physically at the dinner table but mentally reviewing your to-do list. You attend the soccer game but spend half the time on your phone handling "urgent" business.

You tell yourself you're doing it for them, but from their perspective, you're choosing everything else over them.

This isn't about working less necessarily. This is about being more intentional about how you transition between work mode and family mode, and how you protect the time you do have together.

***

The Presence Practice

Being present with your family requires conscious transition from professional mode to personal mode. You can't just walk through the door and expect to instantly be emotionally available after spending all day in a completely different mindset.

Just like you prepare for important work meetings, you need to prepare for important family time. This might mean taking five minutes in your car before going inside to mentally shift gears. It might mean having a ritual that helps you transition from work identity to family identity.

The goal is to show up as intentionally for your family as you do for your most important professional responsibilities.

***

The Memory-Making Mindset

Your children won't remember your quarterly earnings or how many deals you closed. They'll remember Saturday morning pancakes, the time you taught them to ride a bike, and whether you were really listening when they told you about their day.

Your partner won't remember how many hours you worked or how successful you looked to others. They'll remember whether you were emotionally available during difficult conversations, whether you celebrated their wins, and whether they felt like a priority in your life.

The moments that create lasting memories are usually ordinary moments where you chose to be fully present instead of distracted.

This doesn't mean you need to manufacture special experiences constantly. It means you need to recognize that ordinary moments become special when you bring your full attention to them.

***

The Identity Integration at Home

Remember your "I Am" statement? Your family should experience those qualities more than anyone else, not less.

If you've identified yourself as a compassionate leader, your children should experience your compassion and your leadership. If you see yourself as encouraging and supportive, your partner should feel encouraged and supported by you.

Too many people save their best qualities for professional contexts and default to whoever's convenient at home. But your family relationships should be where your authentic identity shines most brightly, not where it disappears.

***

The Energy Investment Strategy

The best family time happens when you're energized, not when you're depleted. This means being strategic about when and how you engage with your family.

Instead of giving them whatever energy remains after work, consider giving them some of your best energy. This might mean having meaningful conversations in the morning when you're fresh rather than trying to connect when you're exhausted.

It might mean protecting certain times of day or week for family focus, when work isn't allowed to intrude.

It might mean being more efficient with work so you have more energy available for the people who matter most.

***

The Long-Term Vision

Think about the kind of family legacy you want to create. What do you want your children to remember about growing up in your home? What do you want your partner to say about your relationship when they talk to others?

This isn't about being perfect. It's about being intentional.

Do you want to be remembered as someone who was always busy, always stressed, always somewhere else mentally? Or do you want to be remembered as someone who made them feel valued, heard, and prioritized?

Do you want your children to learn that success requires sacrificing relationships? Or do you want them to see that it's possible to be successful at work while still being present at home?

***

The Boundaries That Matter

Protecting family time requires boundaries. This means sometimes saying no to work opportunities, client demands, or social obligations that would interfere with the moments that matter most.

It means having clear rules about when work is allowed to interrupt family time and when it's not. It means communicating to others that your family time is as important as your work time.

This doesn't mean being rigid or never being flexible. It means being intentional about what you protect and why.

***

Your Daily Challenge: Family Vision Design

Today, you're going to create a clear vision for how you want to show up in your family relationships and what kind of family life you want to build.

Step 1: Current Family Presence Assessment Honestly evaluate how you currently show up at home:

- What percentage of family time are you mentally present vs. distracted?

- What energy level do you typically bring to family interactions?

- How does your family currently experience your priorities?

- When you're home, are you really home?

Step 2: The Memory Audit Think about your favorite family memories:

- What made those moments special?

- What was different about your presence during those times?

- What do these memories tell you about what your family values most?

Step 3: The Identity Integration Check Consider how your authentic identity should show up at home:

- How should your family experience the qualities from your "I Am" statement?

- What leadership qualities should your children see in you?

- How should your partner experience your core values?

Step 4: The Family Vision Creation Design your ideal family life:

- How do you want to be present during family time?

- What kind of atmosphere do you want to create at home?

- What traditions or routines would support connection?

- How do you want your family members to feel when they're with you?

Step 5: The Daily Rhythm Design Think about typical family interactions:

- How do you want to transition from work to family time?

- What would make family dinners more meaningful?

- How could bedtime routines become connection opportunities?

- What weekend activities would create lasting memories?

Step 6: The Boundary Planning Identify what you need to protect family time:

- When should work not be allowed to interrupt?

- What boundaries do you need to set with clients or colleagues?

- How will you handle "urgent" requests during family time?

- What would need to change to give your family your best energy?

Step 7: The Legacy Vision Think long-term about the family legacy you want to create:

- What do you want your children to remember about their childhood?

- How do you want your partner to describe your relationship?

- What values do you want to model through your presence?

- What would you regret not doing if you continue your current patterns?

Step 8: The Integration Plan Based on your vision, identify specific changes:

- What's one way you could be more present during family time this week?

- How could you better transition from work mode to family mode?

- What family tradition or routine could you start or improve?

- What boundary do you need to establish to protect family time?

The goal isn't to become a perfect family member overnight. The goal is to start being as intentional about your family relationships as you are about your professional success.

Your family didn't sign up to get the leftover version of who you are. They deserve to experience the same engaged, authentic, energetic person that everyone else gets to see.

When you bring your best self home instead of saving it for work, your family relationships become a source of energy rather than something that competes with your other priorities.

Tomorrow, we'll explore what personal growth looks like in an integrated life. But today, focus on designing family relationships that reflect your authentic identity and values.

Because at the end of your life, your family relationships will matter more than any professional achievement. Make sure you're investing accordingly.

FOURTEEN

Day 13: Personal Growth Goals

Who are you becoming?

Most people approach personal growth like they're trying to fix something broken. They identify their weaknesses, their problem areas, their character flaws, and then create improvement plans to become better versions of themselves.

But what if personal growth isn't about fixing what's wrong with you? What if it's about becoming more of who you already are at your best?

The most integrated people don't grow by trying to become someone entirely different. They grow by amplifying their authentic qualities, developing their natural strengths, and becoming more consistent in living out their core identity.

This isn't about avoiding growth or accepting mediocrity. This is about growing in alignment with who you actually are rather than trying to become who you think you should be.

***

The Authentic Growth Model

Traditional personal development tells you to identify your weaknesses and work on fixing them. But we've already established that focusing on weaknesses is energy-draining and rarely produces lasting change.

Authentic growth focuses on becoming more of who you are when you're operating at your best. It's about increasing the frequency and consistency of your peak moments rather than trying to eliminate your struggles.

If you're naturally a compassionate leader, authentic growth means becoming more consistently compassionate and more effectively leading. If you're naturally creative and innovative, growth means expanding your creative capacity and finding better outlets for innovation.

This doesn't mean ignoring areas where you need to improve. It means approaching improvement from a place of strength rather than deficiency.

***

The Identity Evolution Process

Remember your "I Am" statement from Day 6? Personal growth is about evolving that identity - not replacing it, but expanding it.

If your current identity is "I am a bold and compassionate leader," growth might involve becoming more consistently bold in difficult situations, or developing more nuanced ways to express compassion, or expanding your leadership capacity to influence larger circles.

The core of who you are doesn't change. The expression and impact of who you are deepens and expands.

This is completely different from trying to become someone you're not. It's about becoming a more developed version of who you already are.

***

The Integration Growth Challenge

For people living integrated lives, personal growth has to work across all areas simultaneously. You can't compartmentalize growth into just professional development or just personal improvement.

Any growth goal you set should enhance your ability to show up authentically everywhere. It should make you better at work AND better at home AND better in your relationships AND better for your own well-being.

If a growth goal only helps you professionally but makes you worse as a parent or partner, it's not authentic growth - it's just another way to fragment yourself.

***

The Character vs. Skills Distinction

There are two types of growth: character development and skill acquisition. Both matter, but character development is more fundamental.

Skills are external capabilities - learning new technologies, developing better communication techniques, improving your physical fitness, mastering new professional competencies.

Character is internal qualities - becoming more patient, developing deeper integrity, increasing your capacity for courage, growing in wisdom and discernment.

Skills help you do things better. Character helps you be someone better.

The most sustainable growth focuses primarily on character development, with skills supporting who you're becoming rather than defining it.

***

The Sustainable Growth Principle

The best personal growth goals are ones you can maintain while living an integrated life. They should enhance your energy rather than drain it. They should make your other priorities easier rather than harder.

If your growth goals require you to sacrifice sleep, neglect relationships, or abandon other important areas of your life, they're not sustainable. Eventually, you'll have to choose between growth and the rest of your life.

Sustainable growth integrates naturally into your existing rhythms and responsibilities. It makes you better at everything you're already committed to rather than adding overwhelming new commitments.

***

The Compound Effect Vision

Think about who you could become if you consistently grew in small ways over the next five years. Not dramatic transformation, but steady development of your authentic qualities.

If you became 10% more consistent in living your values each year, where would you be in five years?

If you developed your natural strengths by 15% annually, how would that change your impact?

If you became slightly more integrated - more of the same person everywhere you go - each year, what would that compound into over time?

Small, consistent growth in alignment with who you are creates massive compound effects over time.

***

The Growth Without Guilt Model

Many people approach personal growth with guilt as motivation. They focus on all the ways they're falling short and use shame to drive improvement.

But guilt-driven growth rarely lasts because it's based on trying to escape negative feelings rather than moving toward positive vision.

Authentic growth is driven by excitement about who you're becoming rather than shame about who you are. It's pulled forward by vision rather than pushed by guilt.

This doesn't mean being satisfied with mediocrity. It means being motivated by possibility rather than inadequacy.

***

Your Daily Challenge: Authentic Growth Design

Today, you're going to design personal growth goals that amplify your authentic identity rather than trying to fix what's "wrong" with you.

Step 1: Peak Moment Analysis Think about times when you were operating at your absolute best:

- What qualities were you expressing most strongly?

- What made those moments different from your typical experience?

- When do you feel most like the person described in your "I Am" statement?

- What conditions bring out your best self?

Step 2: Consistency Gap Identification Consider the difference between your peak self and your typical self:

- Which of your best qualities show up inconsistently?

- What prevents you from operating at your best more often?

- Where do you fall short of your own "I Am" statement?

- What would need to change for you to be more consistently authentic?

Step 3: Character Development Focus Identify 2-3 character qualities you want to develop:

- Which aspects of your core identity could be stronger?

- What internal qualities would make you better everywhere you show up?

- What character development would enhance all your relationships?

- What would make you more consistently the person you want to be?

Step 4: Skill Enhancement Selection Choose 1-2 skills that would support your character development:

- What capabilities would help you express your authentic identity better?

- What skills would make you more effective in your areas of strength?

- What would help you have greater impact through your natural abilities?

- What learning would serve your integrated life across multiple areas?

Step 5: Integration Check For each growth goal, verify it supports your whole life:

- Will this make you better at work AND at home?

- Does this align with your core values and identity?

- Will this enhance your energy or drain it?

- Can you pursue this growth while maintaining your other priorities?

Step 6: The Compound Vision Imagine yourself five years from now if you consistently grew in these areas:

- Who would you become if you developed these character qualities?

- How would this growth change your impact on others?

- What would be possible in your life if you became this person?

- How would this serve your integrated life vision?

Step 7: Sustainable Implementation Planning Design how you'll actually grow in these areas:

- What small, daily practices would develop these qualities?

- How will you measure progress in character development?

- What learning or skill development fits your current schedule?

- How will you maintain these growth practices long-term?

Step 8: The Growth Commitment Write a commitment statement that captures your growth vision: "I commit to becoming more consistently _____ by developing _____ through _____."

Example: "I commit to becoming more consistently compassionate and bold by developing my patience and courage through daily reflection and weekly challenging conversations."

The goal isn't to become someone entirely different. The goal is to become more consistently and effectively who you already are at your best.

Personal growth should feel like coming home to yourself, not like trying to become someone else.

Tomorrow, we'll put together your complete life vision by integrating everything you've discovered this week. But today, focus on growth that amplifies your authentic identity rather than fighting against it.

Because the world doesn't need you to become someone else. The world needs you to become more fully yourself.

FIFTEEN

Day 14: Your Complete Life Vision

Putting it all together into one clear picture

You've spent the last week clearing mental clutter, designing your ideal Monday, envisioning better relationships, reimagining work that serves your whole life, creating meaningful family dynamics, and planning authentic personal growth.

Now it's time to weave all of those individual pieces into one coherent vision of your integrated life.

This isn't about creating a perfect fantasy that will never happen. This is about painting a clear picture of what becomes possible when you consistently live from your authentic identity across all areas of your life.

Your complete life vision is your North Star. It's the reference point for every decision you make and every choice about how to spend your time and energy.

***

The Integration Test

A truly integrated life vision has a consistent thread running through every area. The same core identity, values, and authentic qualities show up in your work, your relationships, your personal growth, and your daily rhythms.

You shouldn't need to be different people in different contexts. The person who shows up at work should be the same person who shows up at home, who shows up with friends, who shows up for personal challenges.

This doesn't mean you act identically in every situation. It means your fundamental character, your core values, and your authentic energy remain consistent regardless of the context.

When your vision passes the integration test, living it becomes energizing rather than exhausting because you're not constantly switching between different versions of yourself.

***

The Authentic Sustainability Check

Your complete life vision should feel sustainable and authentic, not like something you have to strain to maintain.

If your vision requires you to be someone you're not, it won't last. If it demands perfection or requires you to have unlimited energy, it will collapse under pressure.

The best life visions are natural extensions of who you already are at your best. They feel like "yes, this is exactly who I want to be and how I want to live" rather than "I hope I can somehow become this person."

***

The Whole Life Coherence

Each area of your vision should support and enhance the other areas rather than competing with them.

Your work vision should make your family life easier, not harder. Your personal growth goals should make you better at work and at home. Your relationship dynamics should give you energy for everything else you want to accomplish.

When all the pieces work together, you create upward spirals where success in one area creates more capacity for success in other areas.

***

The Decision Filter Framework

Your complete life vision becomes a powerful decision-making tool. When you're clear on the integrated life you're building, choices become much simpler.

Does this opportunity move you toward your vision or away from it? Does this commitment align with the person you're becoming or does it require you to be someone you're not? Will saying yes to this support your integrated life or fragment it?

You stop making decisions based on what looks good to others, what pays the most, or what feels urgent in the moment. You start making decisions based on what serves the coherent life you're intentionally building.

***

The Energy Alignment Principle

Your complete vision should energize you when you think about it. Not in a manic, unsustainable way, but in a deep, resonant way that makes you think "yes, this is worth working toward."

If your vision feels overwhelming, it's probably too complex or not authentic enough. If it feels boring, it's probably not challenging enough or not aligned with what you actually want.

The right vision feels like a natural expression of who you are combined with exciting growth toward who you're becoming.

**

Your Daily Challenge: Complete Vision Integration

Today, you're going to synthesize everything from this week into one coherent picture of your integrated life.

Step 1: Identity Foundation Review Start with your core identity from Week 1:

- What is your "I Am" statement?

- What are your core values and non-negotiables?

- What are your primary strengths and energy patterns?

- What does authenticity feel like for you?

Step 2: Vision Elements Compilation Gather your vision work from this week:

- Your ideal Monday design

- How you want to show up in relationships

- What work that works looks like for you

- Your family life vision

- Your authentic growth goals

Step 3: The Integration Weaving Look for the common threads across all areas:

- How does your core identity show up in each area?

- Where do you see your values consistently expressed?

- What authentic qualities appear throughout your vision?

- How do the different areas support each other?

Step 4: The Complete Picture Writing Write a comprehensive description of your integrated life vision. Include:

Daily Rhythms: How do you typically structure your days? What energy do you bring to your daily routines?

Work Integration: How does your work reflect your identity and serve your whole life? What impact are you having professionally?

Relationship Dynamics: How do you show up with the people who matter most? What kind of presence do you bring to your relationships?

Family Life: How are you present for the moments that matter? What kind of family legacy are you creating?

Personal Growth: Who are you becoming? How are you developing your authentic qualities?

Overall Integration: How does being the same person everywhere make your life more energizing and effective?

Step 5: The Sustainability Check Review your complete vision and ask:

- Does this feel like a natural expression of who I am?

- Can I maintain this without burning out or becoming someone I'm not?

- Do all the pieces work together rather than competing with each other?

- Does this energize me when I think about living it?

Step 6: The Decision Filter Creation Based on your vision, create decision-making criteria:

- What questions will you ask before saying yes to new opportunities?

- How will you evaluate whether choices align with your integrated life?

- What boundaries do you need to maintain to protect this vision?

Step 7: The One-Year Milestone Imagine yourself one year from now living this integrated life:

- What would be different about your daily experience?

- How would others describe the change in you?

- What would you have accomplished by staying true to this vision?

- How would you feel about the direction of your life?

Step 8: The Commitment Declaration Write a commitment statement that captures your intention to live this integrated life:

"I commit to building a life where I am the same authentic person everywhere I go, where my work serves my whole life, where my relationships reflect my best qualities, and where my growth makes me more of who I am at my core."

Step 9: The Vision Summary Distill your complete vision into 2-3 paragraphs that capture the essence of the integrated life you're building. This becomes your reference point for all future decisions.

The goal isn't to create a perfect plan that you'll execute flawlessly. The goal is to have a clear picture of what you're building so you can make consistent choices that move you in that direction.

Your complete life vision is your declaration of what becomes possible when you refuse to live a fragmented life. It's your commitment to showing up as yourself everywhere you go and building something coherent and meaningful with your time on earth.

This week, you've moved from asking "Who am I?" to declaring "This is what I'm building with who I am."

Next week, we'll take an honest look at where you currently are so you can create a realistic plan to bridge the gap between your current reality and your integrated vision.

But today, celebrate the clarity you've created. You now know what you're working toward. That puts you ahead of 95% of people who are just reacting to whatever life throws at them.

You have a vision. Now the real work begins.

SIXTEEN

Day 15: Reality Check

Rating yourself honestly across all life areas

You have a clear vision of your integrated life. You know who you are at your core and what you want to build with that identity. Now comes the part that separates dreamers from people who actually create change: getting brutally honest about where you currently are.

This isn't about beating yourself up or cataloging everything that's wrong with your life. This is about creating an accurate baseline so you can make realistic plans to bridge the gap between your current reality and your vision.

Most people skip this step because it's uncomfortable. They prefer to stay in the fantasy of what they want to create rather than facing the truth about what they're actually living right now.

But you can't navigate from where you want to be - you can only navigate from where you are.

***

The Honesty Requirement

This assessment requires complete honesty, which means admitting things you might not want to face:

- Areas where you're not living up to your own values

- Relationships where you're not showing up as your best self

- Work situations that drain your energy but you've been pretending are fine

- Habits and patterns that contradict your stated priorities

- The gap between who you say you are and how you actually spend your time

The temptation will be to rate yourself higher than reality or to make excuses for why things aren't where you want them to be. Resist that temptation. The more honest you are now, the more effective your planning will be.

***

The Integrated Assessment Model

You're going to rate yourself across all the major areas of life, but not as separate categories. Remember, the goal is integration - being the same authentic person everywhere you go.

As you assess each area, ask yourself: "How consistently am I living my authentic identity in this area? How well does this area of my life reflect my core values and vision?"

This isn't about perfection. This is about alignment and consistency.

***

The Energy Reality Check

For each area, pay attention to your energy:

- Does this area of your life energize you or drain you?

- Are you operating from your strengths or constantly swimming upstream?

- Do you feel authentic in this area or like you're performing?

- Does this area support your other priorities or compete with them?

Energy is often the most honest indicator of how well your current reality aligns with your authentic self.

***

The Time and Attention Audit

Look at where your time and attention actually go, not where you think they go or where you wish they went:

- What percentage of your waking hours is spent on each area?

- Where does your mental energy go throughout the day?

- What gets your best focus and what gets your leftovers?

- How does your actual time allocation compare to your stated priorities?

Time and attention reveal your true priorities, regardless of what you say matters most.

***

The Relationship Reality Assessment

Your relationships are often the clearest mirror of how integrated you actually are:

- Do the people closest to you see your authentic identity or a performed version?

- Are you giving your best energy to the relationships that matter most?

- How present are you when you're with the people you love?

- Do your relationships energize you or drain you?

If there's a significant gap between how you show up professionally and how you show up personally, that's a key indicator of fragmentation.

***

The Values Alignment Check

Compare your daily choices to your core values:

- When did you last compromise a core value for convenience or advantage?

- How often do you make decisions that align with your stated non-negotiables?

- Where are you living in contradiction to what you say matters most?

- What percentage of your choices reflect your authentic identity?

This isn't about judging yourself - it's about identifying where the disconnects are so you can address them.

***

Your Daily Challenge: The Complete Reality Assessment

Today, you're going to honestly assess where you currently are across all areas of your life. Rate each area on a scale of 1-10, where 10 means "completely aligned with my vision and authentic identity" and 1 means "completely disconnected from who I want to be."

Part 1: Professional Reality Rate your current work situation:

- How well does your work reflect your core identity? (1-10)

- How much does your work energize vs. drain you? (1-10)

- How aligned is your work with your values? (1-10)

- How sustainable is your current work approach? (1-10)

- Overall Professional Rating: ___/10

Reality Notes: What's actually happening in your work life that supports or contradicts your vision?

Part 2: Physical Reality Rate your current physical health and energy:

- How well are you managing your energy throughout the day? (1-10)

- How sustainable are your physical habits? (1-10)

- How does your physical state support your other priorities? (1-10)

- How aligned is your physical care with your values? (1-10)

- Overall Physical Rating: ___/10

Reality Notes: What's actually happening with your physical health and energy management?

Part 3: Financial Reality Rate your current financial situation:

- How aligned is your money management with your values? (1-10)

- How much stress vs. peace does money create in your life? (1-10)

- How well do your financial choices support your integrated vision? (1-10)

- How sustainable are your current financial patterns? (1-10)

- Overall Financial Rating: ___/10

Reality Notes: What's actually happening with your financial choices and stress levels?

Part 4: Relational Reality Rate your current relationships:

- How authentically do you show up in your closest relationships? (1-10)

- How much energy do your relationships give vs. take? (1-10)

- How present are you when you're with people who matter? (1-10)

- How well do your relationships reflect your core identity? (1-10)

- Overall Relational Rating: ___/10

Reality Notes: What's actually happening in your most important relationships?

Part 5: Emotional Reality Rate your current emotional health:

- How well do you manage stress and emotional challenges? (1-10)

- How authentic are you about your emotional needs? (1-10)

- How sustainable is your current emotional state? (1-10)

- How much does your emotional health support your other areas? (1-10)

- Overall Emotional Rating: ___/10

Reality Notes: What's actually happening with your emotional well-being and stress management?

Part 6: Spiritual Reality Rate your current spiritual/meaning-making life:

- How connected do you feel to your deeper purpose? (1-10)

- How aligned are your daily choices with your spiritual values? (1-10)

- How much meaning and fulfillment do you experience? (1-10)

- How does your spiritual life support your integrated vision? (1-10)

- Overall Spiritual Rating: ___/10

Reality Notes: What's actually happening with your sense of purpose and meaning?

Part 7: Integration Reality Check Rate your overall integration:

- How consistent is your identity across different areas? (1-10)

- How well do all areas of your life work together? (1-10)

- How authentic do you feel in your daily life? (1-10)

- How sustainable is your current overall approach? (1-10)

- Overall Integration Rating: ___/10

Part 8: The Honest Summary Calculate your averages:

- Total points across all six areas: ___/60

- Overall average: ___/10

- Highest rated area: _____

- Lowest rated area: _____

- Biggest gap between vision and reality: _____

Part 9: The Reality Acceptance Write a brief, honest summary of where you actually are right now:

- What's working well that you can build on?

- What are the biggest gaps between your vision and reality?

- Where are you living in contradiction to your stated values?

- What patterns or habits are keeping you stuck?

The goal isn't to judge your scores or feel bad about low ratings. The goal is to have an accurate starting point for the planning work you'll do this week.

Tomorrow, you'll analyze the gap between your vision and reality to identify the most important areas to focus on. But today, focus on being completely honest about where you currently are.

Because transformation starts with truth. And truth starts with admitting where you really are, not where you wish you were.

SEVENTEEN

Day 16: Vision vs Reality

Vision vs. reality - what's the difference?

Yesterday, you took an honest look at where you currently are. Today, you're going to compare that reality to the vision you created last week and identify exactly where the gaps are.

This is where most people get overwhelmed. They see the distance between where they are and where they want to be, and it feels impossible. The gap seems too big, the changes too dramatic, the timeline too long.

But here's what separates people who actually transform their lives from people who just dream about it: they break down overwhelming gaps into manageable pieces and focus on the most important changes first.

You don't have to close every gap simultaneously. You just have to identify which gaps matter most and start there.

***

The Gap Analysis Framework

A gap isn't just "I want this and I don't have it." There are different types of gaps, and each requires a different approach:

Skills Gaps: You know what to do but don't know how to do it

Habit Gaps: You know what to do and how to do it, but you're not doing it consistently

Belief Gaps: Part of you doesn't believe the change is possible or worth it

System Gaps: Your current environment or structures don't support the change

Energy Gaps: You don't have the physical or emotional resources to sustain the change

Priority Gaps: Other things are taking precedence over what you say matters most

Identifying the type of gap helps you choose the right strategy to close it.

***

The Overwhelm Trap

When you look at all the areas where your reality doesn't match your vision, it's easy to feel like everything needs to change immediately. This leads to the classic overwhelm trap where you try to transform your entire life at once and end up changing nothing.

The solution isn't to lower your vision or accept mediocrity. The solution is to be strategic about which changes will create the biggest impact on your integrated life.

Some gaps are foundational - closing them makes everything else easier. Other gaps are surface-level - they're noticeable but don't affect your ability to make progress in other areas.

Your job is to identify the foundational gaps and focus your energy there first.

***

The Compound Effect Principle

The best gap analysis identifies changes that create positive ripple effects across multiple areas of your life.

For example, if you improve your energy management (physical area), you'll have more capacity for better relationships, more effective work, and more consistent personal growth. One improvement supports everything else.

Conversely, some gaps are isolated - closing them only improves that specific area without affecting anything else. These gaps might be worth addressing eventually, but they shouldn't be your first priority.

Look for gaps where improvement in one area would naturally support improvement in others.

***

The Identity Alignment Priority

Remember, the goal isn't just to improve individual areas of your life. The goal is to live more consistently from your authentic identity across all areas.

The most important gaps to address are those where you're not showing up as the person described in your "I Am" statement. These identity misalignments create internal conflict and make everything else harder.

If your identity includes being a compassionate leader, but you're consistently impatient with your family, that's a foundational gap that affects your ability to feel authentic anywhere.

If your identity includes being bold and courageous, but you're avoiding difficult conversations at work, that contradiction will undermine your confidence in every area of your life.

***

The Energy Economics of Change

Every change requires energy to initiate and maintain. You have limited energy, so you need to be strategic about how you invest it.

Changes that align with your natural strengths and energy patterns require less ongoing energy to maintain. Changes that go against your nature require constant effort and willpower.

When analyzing gaps, consider: "If I made this change, would it give me more energy for other changes, or would it drain energy I need for other priorities?"

The best first changes are ones that create more energy than they consume.

***

Your Daily Challenge: Strategic Gap Identification

Today, you're going to systematically analyze the gaps between your vision and reality to identify which ones to focus on first.

Step 1: Gap Inventory For each area you assessed yesterday, identify the specific gaps:

Professional Gaps:

- What's the difference between your ideal work situation and your current reality?

- What would need to change for your work to fully support your integrated life?

- List 3-5 specific professional gaps.

Physical Gaps:

- What's the difference between your ideal energy/health and your current state?

- What habits or systems would need to change?

- List 3-5 specific physical gaps.

Financial Gaps:

- What's the difference between your ideal financial situation and current reality?

- What money habits or decisions would need to change?

- List 3-5 specific financial gaps.

Relational Gaps:

- What's the difference between how you want to show up in relationships and how you currently show up?

- Which relationships need the most attention?

- List 3-5 specific relational gaps.

Emotional Gaps:

- What's the difference between your ideal emotional health and your current patterns?

- What would need to change about how you handle stress and emotions?

- List 3-5 specific emotional gaps.

Spiritual Gaps:

- What's the difference between your ideal sense of purpose/meaning and your current experience?

- What would need to change about how you connect with deeper values?

- List 3-5 specific spiritual gaps.

Step 2: Gap Type Classification For each gap you identified, determine what type it is:

- Skills Gap (don't know how)

- Habit Gap (know how but not doing)

- Belief Gap (don't believe it's possible/worth it)

- System Gap (environment doesn't support it)

- Energy Gap (don't have resources)

- Priority Gap (other things taking precedence)

Step 3: Impact Assessment Rate each gap on two factors:

- Impact on Integration (1-10): How much would closing this gap improve your ability to live authentically across all areas?

- Ripple Effect (1-10): How much would closing this gap make other improvements easier?

Step 4: Identity Alignment Check For each gap, ask: "Is this gap preventing me from consistently living my 'I Am' statement?" Mark gaps that create identity misalignment as high priority.

Step 5: Energy Economics Analysis For each gap, consider:

- How much energy would it take to close this gap?

- Would closing this gap give me more energy for other changes?

- Does this align with my natural strengths and patterns?

Step 6: The Strategic Priority Matrix Plot your gaps on this matrix:

High Impact + High Ripple Effect = FOUNDATIONAL (Focus here first) High Impact + Low Ripple Effect = IMPORTANT (Address after foundational) Low Impact + High Ripple Effect = STRATEGIC (Consider for momentum) Low Impact + Low Ripple Effect = EVENTUAL (Address last if at all)

Step 7: Top 5 Gap Selection Based on your analysis, identify the 5 most important gaps to focus on:

1. _____ (Type: _____ Impact: __ Ripple: __)

2. _____ (Type: _____ Impact: __ Ripple: __)

3. _____ (Type: _____ Impact: __ Ripple: __)

4. _____ (Type: _____ Impact: __ Ripple: __)

5. _____ (Type: _____ Impact: __ Ripple: __)

Step 8: The Reality Check For your top 5 gaps, honestly assess:

- Can you realistically work on all 5 simultaneously?

- Which 1-2 would create the biggest positive change if you focused there first?

- What would need to be true about your current life to successfully close these gaps?

Step 9: The Focus Decision Choose your ONE primary focus gap - the single most important change that would have the biggest impact on your integrated life.

My Primary Focus Gap:
_____

Why this gap matters most:

_____

How closing this gap would improve my whole life: _____

The goal isn't to create a perfect improvement plan for every area of your life. The goal is to identify the most strategic place to focus your change energy first.

Tomorrow, you'll look at what's already working in your life that you can build on. But today, focus on getting clear about where the most important improvements need to happen.

Because clarity about your gaps is the foundation for strategic change. And strategic change is the only kind that actually lasts.

EIGHTEEN

Day 17: What's Already Working

Don't throw the baby out with the bathwater

When people get focused on what needs to change in their lives, they often make a critical mistake: they assume everything needs to be different. They throw out what's working along with what's broken, and end up making their transformation journey much harder than it needs to be.

But here's the truth: you already have parts of your life that align with your vision and reflect your authentic identity. You already have habits, relationships, and practices that energize you rather than drain you. You already have areas where you're showing up consistently as the person you want to be.

These aren't accidents. They're clues about what works with your natural wiring and what you can build on rather than rebuild from scratch.

Today is about identifying what's already working so you can amplify it rather than accidentally destroy it while trying to fix everything else.

***

The Foundation Principle

Think of your life like a house that needs renovation. Before you start tearing down walls and ripping out systems, you need to identify which parts of the structure are solid and can support the improvements you want to make.

The parts of your life that are already working are your foundation. They're proof that you can live aligned with your authentic identity. They show you what's possible when your choices match your values and your energy flows in the right direction.

Instead of starting from zero, you're going to identify these foundation elements and use them as the base for everything else you want to build.

***

The Success Pattern Recognition

The areas where you're already successful contain patterns you can replicate in other areas. They reveal the conditions, habits, and approaches that work best for your unique wiring.

If you're naturally present and engaged with your children but struggle to be present at work, what's different about those contexts? What makes family engagement feel natural while work engagement feels forced?

If you're consistent with certain habits but inconsistent with others, what makes the consistent habits stick? What support systems, triggers, or rewards are built into those patterns?

If certain relationships energize you while others drain you, what's different about how you show up or what you bring to each interaction?

Your successes aren't random. They're data about what works for you.

***

The Energy Source Identification

Pay special attention to the areas of your life that give you energy rather than taking it. These are gold mines of insight about how to structure other areas of your life.

The activities that energize you reveal your natural strengths in action. The relationships that energize you show you what authentic connection looks like for you. The environments that energize you tell you what conditions support your best performance.

Instead of trying to force yourself to thrive in contexts that drain you, you can learn from the contexts that energize you and either modify the draining areas or structure your life to include more of what works.

***

The Values Alignment Audit

Look for areas where your current choices already align with your core values. These are often the areas where decisions feel easy and natural because you're not fighting against what you believe is right.

Maybe you're already excellent at maintaining integrity in your business relationships. Maybe you're already consistent in putting family first when it really matters. Maybe you're already good at investing in personal growth or managing your physical health.

These aligned areas don't need to be fixed - they need to be celebrated and protected as you work on the areas that need improvement.

The Identity Consistency Check

Remember your "I Am" statement? Look for areas where you're already living that identity consistently. These are proof points that your authentic self can show up powerfully in real-world contexts.

If your identity includes being a compassionate leader, where are you already leading with compassion effectively? If you see yourself as someone who empowers others, where are you already doing that well?

These aren't areas to change - they're areas to maintain and potentially expand while you work on bringing that same authentic identity to other contexts.

***

The Relationship Success Analysis

Your relationships often reveal where you're already showing up authentically. Look for relationships where you feel energized, valued, and able to be completely yourself.

What's different about these relationships? How do you show up differently? What do these relationships bring out in you that others don't?

These relationship patterns can be templates for improving other relationships rather than starting from scratch with new relationship skills.

***

Your Daily Challenge: Success Pattern Mining

Today, you're going to systematically identify what's already working in your life so you can build on it rather than accidentally undermining it.

Step 1: Energy Source Inventory Identify activities, relationships, and contexts that consistently give you energy:

- What parts of your work energize you?

- Which relationships leave you feeling more alive?

- What daily or weekly activities do you look forward to?

- What environments make you feel most like yourself?

- When do you feel most authentic and confident?

Step 2: Success Pattern Analysis For each area you assessed earlier, identify what's already working:

Professional Success Patterns:

- What aspects of your work align with your strengths?

- When do you feel most effective and authentic professionally?

- What work relationships or dynamics are already healthy?

Physical Success Patterns:

- What health or energy habits are you already consistent with?

- When do you feel most physically capable and strong?

- What physical activities or routines work well for you?

Financial Success Patterns:

- What financial habits or decisions already align with your values?

- Where do you already feel confident and wise with money?

- What financial systems or approaches are working?

Relational Success Patterns:

- Which relationships already reflect your authentic identity?

- Where are you already showing up as your best self with others?

- What relationship dynamics energize rather than drain you?

Emotional Success Patterns:

- What emotional management strategies already work for you?

- When do you handle stress or challenges most effectively?

- What emotional habits or practices support your well-being?

Spiritual Success Patterns:

- Where do you already feel connected to your deeper purpose?

- What practices or experiences already provide meaning and fulfillment?

- When do you feel most aligned with your core values?

Step 3: Values Alignment Identification For each area, identify where your current choices already align with your core values:

- Where are you already living your non-negotiables consistently?

- What decisions feel natural and right because they match your values?

- Where do you already have good boundaries that protect what matters most?

Step 4: Identity Consistency Recognition Identify where you're already living your "I Am" statement effectively:

- Where does your authentic identity already show up powerfully?

- What contexts bring out the qualities described in your identity statement?

- Where are you already being the person you want to be consistently?

Step 5: Foundation Element Categorization Organize what you've discovered into categories:

Strong Foundations (8-10 rating from your reality check):

- What's working so well it just needs to be maintained?

Good Foundations (6-7 rating):

- What's working pretty well and could be optimized?

Emerging Foundations (4-5 rating):

- What shows promise and could be developed?

Step 6: Replication Strategy Development For your strongest success patterns, identify what makes them work:

- What conditions support these successes?

- What habits or systems are built into these areas?

- How could you replicate these conditions in areas that need improvement?

Step 7: Protection Planning Identify what you need to protect as you work on other changes:

- What successful patterns could be accidentally disrupted by other improvements?

- What relationships or habits need to be maintained during your growth process?

- How will you ensure your changes build on rather than undermine what's working?

Step 8: Amplification Opportunities Look for ways to expand what's already working:

- How could you do more of what's already energizing you?

- Where could you bring successful patterns from one area into another area?

- What working relationships or habits could be strengthened or expanded?

Step 9: Confidence Building Recognition Write a brief appreciation of what you've already accomplished:

- What evidence do you have that you can live authentically and successfully?

- Where have you already proven you can align your choices with your values?

- What gives you confidence that further integration is possible?

The goal isn't to become complacent about areas that are working well. The goal is to recognize that you already have proof of concept for integrated living, and you can build on that foundation rather than starting from scratch.

Tomorrow, you'll identify your biggest obstacles to progress. But today, focus on celebrating and learning from what's already working in your life.

Because transformation isn't about becoming someone entirely different. It's about becoming more consistently who you already are at your best.

NINETEEN

Day 18: Your Biggest Obstacles

What's actually standing in your way?

You know who you are. You have a clear vision of your integrated life. You've identified the gaps between where you are and where you want to be. You've recognized what's already working that you can build on.

Now comes the hard question: What's actually preventing you from closing those gaps and living the life you've envisioned?

Most people never ask this question honestly, so they keep running into the same obstacles over and over again. They try different strategies, read different books, and make different plans, but they never address the root issues that keep sabotaging their progress.

Today is about getting brutally honest about what's really standing in your way so you can deal with those obstacles directly instead of pretending they don't exist.

***

The Real vs. Perceived Obstacle Problem

There's often a big difference between what people think is stopping them and what's actually stopping them.

People think they need more time, but the real obstacle is that they're not protecting the time they have.

People think they need more money, but the real obstacle is that they're not making strategic choices with the resources they have.

People think they need more support, but the real obstacle is that they're not asking for help or accepting the support that's available.

People think they need more motivation, but the real obstacle is that they're trying to change too many things at once and burning out.

The perceived obstacles keep you focused on things you can't control. The real obstacles are usually things you can influence once you identify them clearly.

***

The Internal vs. External Obstacle Matrix

Obstacles fall into two categories, and you need different strategies to address each:

External Obstacles: Things in your environment, circumstances, or relationships that make change difficult
Internal Obstacles: Things in your mindset, habits, or patterns that sabotage your progress

External obstacles often feel more significant because they're visible and concrete. But internal obstacles are usually more limiting because they affect how you respond to every external challenge.

You might think your biggest obstacle is a demanding boss, but if you're conflict-avoidant, that internal pattern will create problems with any boss, not just the current one.

You might think your biggest obstacle is lack of time, but if you consistently over-commit and can't say no, you'll have time problems regardless of your schedule.

***

The System vs. Personal Obstacle Analysis

Some obstacles are about the systems and structures in your life, while others are about personal patterns and choices.

System Obstacles: Your environment, schedule, relationships, or circumstances don't support the changes you want to make

Personal Obstacles: Your habits, mindset, skills, or patterns prevent you from making effective use of the opportunities you have

System obstacles require environmental changes. Personal obstacles require personal development. Trying to solve a system problem with personal effort (or vice versa) is exhausting and ineffective.

***

The Hidden Obstacle Investigation

The most limiting obstacles are often the ones you don't consciously recognize because they've become so normal you don't notice them anymore.

Maybe you automatically say yes to every request because you've never questioned that pattern.

Maybe you consistently underestimate how long things take because you've never tracked your actual time usage.

Maybe you avoid difficult conversations because you've convinced yourself that conflict is always destructive.

Maybe you procrastinate on important changes because you've learned to equate discomfort with danger.

These hidden patterns operate in the background, sabotaging your progress without you realizing it.

***

The Fear-Based Obstacle Category

Many obstacles that look practical are actually fear-based. The fear isn't always obvious - it often disguises itself as reasonable caution or logical concerns.

"I don't have time" might really mean "I'm afraid that if I focus on this, something else important will fall apart."

"I need to research more before I start" might really mean "I'm afraid of making the wrong choice or looking foolish."

"My family wouldn't understand" might really mean "I'm afraid of disapproval or conflict if I change."

"It's not the right time" might really mean "I'm afraid that if I try and fail, I'll prove I'm not capable of change."

Fear-based obstacles require different solutions than practical obstacles, but you can't address them if you don't recognize them.

***

The Competing Commitment Problem

Sometimes your biggest obstacle isn't something external - it's an unconscious commitment that competes with your stated goals.

You say you want better work-life integration, but you're unconsciously committed to being seen as indispensable at work.

You say you want to be more present with your family, but you're unconsciously committed to avoiding the discomfort that comes with setting boundaries.

You say you want to live authentically, but you're unconsciously committed to maintaining an image that requires you to perform rather than be genuine.

These competing commitments create internal conflict that sabotages your progress no matter how good your plans are.

***

Your Daily Challenge: Obstacle Identification and Strategy

Today, you're going to identify your real obstacles so you can develop effective strategies to address them.

Step 1: The Obvious Obstacle List Start with what you think is stopping you from living your integrated vision:

- What external circumstances make change difficult?

- What do you feel like you don't have enough of (time, money, support, etc.)?

- What practical barriers seem to block your progress?

- What would need to change in your environment for transformation to be easier?

Step 2: The Real Obstacle Investigation For each obvious obstacle, dig deeper:

- Is this actually preventing change, or is it making change inconvenient?

- What would happen if you had to work around this obstacle instead of waiting for it to disappear?

- How much of this obstacle is within your influence vs. completely outside your control?

- What's the real issue underneath this surface obstacle?

Step 3: Internal vs. External Classification Categorize your obstacles:

Internal Obstacles (mindset, habits, patterns):

- What personal patterns consistently sabotage your progress?

- What fears or beliefs limit your willingness to take action?

- What habits or automatic responses work against your stated goals?

External Obstacles (environment, circumstances, relationships):

- What environmental factors make positive choices more difficult?

- What relationship dynamics or expectations create pressure to stay the same?

- What practical constraints genuinely limit your options?

Step 4: System vs. Personal Analysis Further categorize your obstacles:

System Obstacles (need environmental changes):

- What structures or systems in your life don't support your vision?

- What needs to change about your schedule, environment, or circumstances?

Personal Obstacles (need personal development):

- What skills, habits, or mindset shifts do you need to develop?

- What personal patterns do you need to change regardless of external circumstances?

Step 5: Hidden Pattern Recognition Look for obstacles you might not consciously recognize:

- What automatic responses do you have that work against your goals?

- What do you consistently avoid or postpone, and why?

- What patterns from your past might be influencing your current choices?

- What unconscious rules or beliefs might be limiting your options?

Step 6: Fear-Based Obstacle Identification For each obstacle, ask: "What am I afraid would happen if this obstacle didn't exist?"

- What fears might be disguised as practical concerns?

- What discomfort are you avoiding by keeping things the same?

- What risks feel too big to take, even if the potential rewards are significant?

Step 7: Competing Commitment Discovery Look for unconscious commitments that compete with your stated goals:

- What benefits do you get from your current patterns, even if they're not optimal?

- What identity or image are you protecting by avoiding change?

- What do you gain by staying stuck that you'd lose by moving forward?

Step 8: The Top 3 Real Obstacles Based on your analysis, identify your 3 most significant real obstacles:

Obstacle 1: _____

Type: Internal/External + System/Personal

Why this matters most: _____

What this obstacle costs you: _____

Obstacle 2: _____

Type: Internal/External + System/Personal

Why this matters most: _____

What this obstacle costs you: _____

Obstacle 3: _____

Type: Internal/External + System/Personal

Why this matters most: _____

What this obstacle costs you: _____

Step 9: Strategy Development For each of your top 3 obstacles, brainstorm potential approaches:

- If this is a system obstacle, what environmental changes would help?

- If this is a personal obstacle, what skills or mindset shifts would help?

- If this is fear-based, what would make the risk feel more manageable?

- If this involves competing commitments, how could you honor both commitments differently?

Step 10: The Honesty Check Write a brief honest assessment:

- Which obstacles are you using as excuses vs. genuine barriers?

- What obstacles are you most resistant to addressing, and why?

- If your biggest obstacles were removed tomorrow, what would you do differently?

The goal isn't to eliminate all obstacles immediately. The goal is to stop being blindsided by predictable patterns and start developing conscious strategies to work with or around the things that typically derail your progress.

Tomorrow, you'll work on prioritizing what matters most when you can't do everything at once. But today, focus on getting clear about what's really standing in your way.

Because you can't solve problems you won't acknowledge, and you can't strategize around obstacles you don't see clearly.

TWENTY

Day 19: Everything Can't Be Urgent

You've identified the gaps between your vision and reality. You know what's already working and what obstacles stand in your way. Now comes one of the hardest parts of transformation: deciding what to focus on first when everything feels important.

Most people fail at creating lasting change not because they don't know what needs to improve, but because they try to improve everything simultaneously. They treat every gap like an emergency and every improvement like a top priority.

This creates a scattered approach where you make minimal progress in multiple areas instead of significant progress in the areas that matter most.

Today is about getting ruthlessly clear on what deserves your attention first, so you can make real progress instead of just staying busy with improvement activities.

**

The Everything-Is-Important Trap

When you're living a fragmented life, everything feels urgent because nothing is working well. Your work demands immediate attention. Your relationships need help. Your health requires focus. Your finances need organizing. Your personal growth feels pressing.

But urgency and importance aren't the same thing. And when everything is important, nothing is actually important - you're just reacting to whatever screams loudest at the moment.

Priority ranking forces you to make hard choices about what gets your best energy and attention first. It's about deciding what you're willing to let be "good enough" for now so you can make something else excellent.

**

The Integration Priority Principle

Remember, the goal isn't to fix individual problems in isolation. The goal is to create an integrated life where you're the same authentic person everywhere you go.

This means your highest priorities should be changes that support integration across multiple areas rather than improvements that only affect one area of your life.

If improving your energy management would make you better at work, more present with your family, and more consistent with personal growth, that's a higher integration priority than learning a new professional skill that only affects your career.

***

The Foundation vs. Surface Distinction

Some changes are foundational - they make everything else easier. Other changes are surface-level - they're nice to have but don't affect your ability to make progress in other areas.

Foundational changes often feel less exciting because they're about systems and habits rather than dramatic results. But they're the changes that compound over time and create sustainable transformation.

Surface changes often feel more motivating because they create visible results quickly. But they're often unsustainable if the foundational issues aren't addressed.

Your highest priorities should be foundational changes that support everything else you want to build.

***

The Energy Economics of Priority Setting

Every change requires energy to initiate and maintain. You have limited energy, so priority ranking is really energy allocation.

Some changes are energy-positive - they give you more energy than they require once they're established. Other changes are energy-neutral or energy-negative - they consistently require energy to maintain.

The highest priority changes are ones that will eventually give you more energy for other improvements. These create upward spirals where each success makes the next success easier.

***

The Compound Effect Timeline

Think about which changes will have the biggest positive impact on your life 12 months from now, not just 12 days from now.

Quick wins can provide motivation, but they don't always translate to long-term transformation. Sustainable changes often require more time to show results but create lasting improvements that compound over time.

Your priority ranking should balance some quicker wins for motivation with longer-term foundational changes that will transform your life over time.

***

The Authenticity Alignment Check

Your highest priorities should be changes that help you live more consistently from your authentic identity. These are changes that reduce the internal conflict between who you are and how you're living.

If your "I Am" statement describes you as a compassionate leader, but you're consistently impatient and reactive in stressful situations, addressing that pattern should be a high priority because it affects your ability to be authentic everywhere.

If your core values include integrity, but your current work requires you to regularly compromise what you believe is right, addressing that misalignment should be prioritized over other improvements.

***

Your Daily Challenge: Strategic Priority Ranking

Today, you're going to rank your improvement opportunities so you can focus your energy where it will have the biggest impact on your integrated life.

Step 1: Complete Improvement Inventory List all the changes you've identified as needed or desired:

- Gaps from your gap analysis (Day 16)

- Areas that need improvement from your reality check (Day 15)

- Obstacles that need to be addressed (Day 18)

- Any other improvements you've been considering

Write them all down - don't edit or prioritize yet, just capture everything.

Step 2: Integration Impact Assessment For each potential change, rate its integration impact (1-10):

- How much would this change help you be more authentically yourself everywhere?

- How much would this improvement support multiple areas of your life?

- How much would this change reduce internal conflict or fragmentation?

Step 3: Foundation vs. Surface Classification Categorize each change:

Foundational Changes (make everything else easier):

- System improvements

- Habit changes

- Mindset shifts

- Energy management improvements

- Core skill development

Surface Changes (nice to have but don't affect other areas):

- Specific goal achievements

- External improvements

- Circumstantial changes

- Cosmetic improvements

Step 4: Energy Economics Analysis For each change, assess:

- Energy Required to Initiate (1-10): How much effort to get started?

- Energy Required to Maintain (1-10): How much ongoing effort?

- Energy Eventually Provided (1-10): How much energy will this give you once established?

Calculate Energy ROI: (Energy Provided - Energy to Maintain) - Energy to Initiate

Step 5: Timeline Impact Evaluation Rate each change on different timelines:

- 30-day impact (1-10): How much difference in one month?

- 6-month impact (1-10): How much difference in six months?

- 2-year impact (1-10): How much difference in two years?

Step 6: Authenticity Alignment Rating For each change, rate (1-10):

- How much would this help you live your "I Am" statement more consistently?

- How much would this reduce the gap between your authentic self and your daily life?

- How much would this allow you to show up as the same person everywhere?

Step 7: Obstacle Removal Priority For changes that address obstacles:

- Which obstacles are preventing multiple other improvements?

- Which obstacles create the most internal conflict or stress?

- Which obstacles, if removed, would make other changes significantly easier?

Step 8: The Strategic Priority Matrix Plot your changes on this matrix based on Integration Impact (x-axis) and Energy ROI (y-axis):

High Integration + High Energy ROI = STRATEGIC PRIORITIES (Focus here first) High Integration + Low Energy ROI = IMPORTANT BUT COSTLY (Plan carefully) Low Integration + High Energy ROI = QUICK WINS (Good for motivation) Low Integration + Low Energy ROI = LOW PRIORITY (Consider not doing)

Step 9: Top 5 Priority Selection Based on your analysis, select your top 5 priorities:

Priority 1: _____

Why this is #1: _____

Integration Impact: ___

Energy ROI: ___

Authenticity Alignment: ___

Priority 2: _____

Why this is #2: _____

Integration Impact: ___

Energy ROI: ___

Authenticity Alignment: ___

Priority 3: _____

Why this is #3: _____

Integration Impact: ___

Energy ROI: ___

Authenticity Alignment: ___

Priority 4: _____

Why this is #4: _____

Integration Impact: ___

Energy ROI: ___

Authenticity Alignment: ___

Priority 5: _____

Why this is #5: _____

Integration Impact: ___

Energy ROI: ___

Authenticity Alignment: ___

Step 10: The Reality Check Answer honestly:

- Can you realistically work on all 5 priorities simultaneously?

- Which 1-2 priorities would create the biggest positive change if you focused there exclusively?

- What would you need to say no to in order to focus on your top priorities?

- How will you resist the temptation to add more priorities once you start making progress?

Step 11: The Focus Decision Choose your ONE primary focus for the next 90 days:

My Primary Focus Priority:
_____

Why this deserves my best energy:
_____

What I'll say no to in order to focus here:
_____

How I'll measure progress:

The goal isn't to create a perfect ranking system or to never adjust your priorities. The goal is to make conscious choices about where your limited energy goes so you can create significant progress rather than scattered improvement.

Tomorrow, you'll choose your single most important focus area and dive deep into understanding it completely. But today, focus on getting clear about what deserves your attention first.

Because trying to change everything changes nothing. But changing the right things in the right order can transform everything.

TWENTY-ONE

Day 20: Your One Thing

The single area that will create the biggest impact

This is the moment that separates people who dream about change from people who actually create it. Everything you've done for the past 19 days has led to this decision: What is the ONE area you're going to focus on first?

Not the five most important areas. Not the three urgent priorities. The ONE single change that will have the biggest impact on your ability to live an integrated, authentic life.

This choice is hard because it requires you to say no to other important improvements - at least for now. It requires you to bet that concentrated effort in one area will be more effective than scattered effort across multiple areas.

But here's what people who successfully transform their lives understand: depth beats breadth every time. Significant progress in one foundational area creates momentum and capacity for progress everywhere else.

**

The Power of Singular Focus

Your brain is not designed for multitasking, especially when it comes to forming new habits or changing established patterns. When you try to focus on multiple changes simultaneously, you dilute your attention and willpower across all of them.

But when you direct all your change energy toward one area, several things happen:

You develop real expertise in managing that type of change, which transfers to other areas later.

You create a success story that builds confidence for tackling other improvements.

You establish systems and processes that can be adapted for other changes.

You free up mental space by not having to track progress in multiple areas.

Most importantly, you actually complete something instead of making minimal progress on everything.

**

The Ripple Effect Principle

The right ONE choice isn't just about improving that single area - it's about choosing the change that will create positive ripples throughout your entire life.

If you choose to focus on energy management, you'll have more capacity for better relationships, more effective work, and more consistent personal growth.

If you choose to focus on authentic communication, you'll improve your work relationships, your family dynamics, and your ability to set boundaries.

If you choose to focus on time boundaries, you'll become more present everywhere and create space for all your other priorities.

The best ONE choice is the change that makes every other change easier.

***

The Foundation vs. Symptom Test

Many people choose to focus on symptoms rather than root causes, which is why their changes don't last.

Symptom focus: "I want to lose 20 pounds" Foundation focus: "I want to develop sustainable energy management habits"

Symptom focus: "I want to make more money" Foundation focus: "I want to align my work with my strengths and values"

Symptom focus: "I want my family to be more supportive" Foundation focus: "I want to show up more authentically in my relationships"

Symptoms are visible and measurable, which makes them feel like obvious choices. But foundation changes address the root causes that create multiple symptoms.

Your ONE choice should be foundational - something that will naturally improve multiple areas of your life.

***

The Authenticity Alignment Priority

Given that your ultimate goal is integration - being the same authentic person everywhere you go - your ONE choice should be the change that most directly supports authentic living.

This might be developing the courage to have difficult conversations if avoiding conflict is keeping you from being genuine.

This might be learning to manage your energy if exhaustion is preventing you from showing up as your best self.

This might be setting better boundaries if over-commitment is fragmenting your attention across too many priorities.

This might be addressing a specific fear or limiting belief if it's preventing you from taking actions aligned with your values.

The question isn't "What would make the biggest difference in my life?" The question is "What would make the biggest difference in my ability to live authentically?"

***

The Readiness Reality Check

Your ONE choice also needs to pass the readiness test. You need to be genuinely ready to commit to this change, not just interested in the idea of it.

Readiness includes:

- Having the time and energy to focus on this change

- Being willing to make trade-offs to prioritize this area

- Having sufficient motivation to push through difficult moments

- Being prepared to maintain focus even when other priorities feel urgent

If you're not truly ready to commit to a change, choosing it as your ONE will just create another failure experience that makes future changes harder.

***

The 90-Day Commitment Frame

Your ONE choice is not forever - it's for your next focused season of change. Think of it as a 90-day commitment to making significant progress in this area before adding other focus areas.

This time frame is long enough to create real change but short enough to maintain focused attention. It's long enough to establish new patterns but short enough that you won't feel trapped if you need to adjust your approach.

Three months of concentrated effort in the right area can create more lasting change than three years of scattered improvement attempts.

**

Your Daily Challenge: The ONE Decision

Today, you make the decision that will determine the trajectory of your transformation journey.

Step 1: Final Priority Review Look back at your top 5 priorities from yesterday:

1.

2.

3.

4.

5.

Step 2: The Ripple Effect Analysis For each of your top 5, honestly assess:

- If you made significant progress in this area, how would it affect your work life?

- How would it affect your family relationships?

- How would it affect your energy and well-being?

- How would it affect your ability to make other changes?

- Which change would create the most positive ripples across all areas?

Step 3: The Foundation Check For each priority, ask:

- Is this addressing a root cause or just a symptom?

- Would progress here naturally improve multiple other areas?

- Is this a foundational change or a surface improvement?

Step 4: The Authenticity Alignment Assessment For each priority, rate (1-10):

- How much would this help me live my "I Am" statement more consistently?

- How much would this reduce the conflict between who I am and how I'm living?

- How directly does this support my ability to be authentic everywhere I go?

Step 5: The Readiness Evaluation For each priority, honestly assess:

- Am I genuinely ready to commit to this change right now?

- Do I have the time and energy to focus here?

- Am I willing to say no to other improvements to prioritize this?

- What would I need to sacrifice or rearrange to make progress here?

Step 6: The Expertise Transfer Consideration Think about which change would teach you skills that transfer to other areas:

- Which focus would develop change management skills I could use elsewhere?

- Which would create systems and processes I could adapt for other improvements?

- Which would build confidence and momentum for future changes?

Step 7: The Fear and Resistance Check Notice which option you're most resistant to choosing:

- What change feels most challenging or uncomfortable?

- What are you afraid might happen if you focus there?

- Is there a change you keep avoiding that might be the most important?

- Sometimes the change you're most resistant to is the one you most need to make.

Step 8: The Gut Check Decision Set aside all the analysis and ask your intuition:

- When you imagine focusing all your change energy on one area, which one feels most right?

- Which change would you be most excited to achieve?

- Which change would make you most proud of yourself?

- Which change aligns most with who you're becoming?

Step 9: The ONE Declaration Based on everything above, choose your ONE focus for the next 90 days:

MY ONE FOCUS:

Why this is the right choice:

How this will create ripple effects in other areas:

What I'm willing to sacrifice to focus here:

How I'll know I'm making progress:

Step 10: The Commitment Ceremony Write and sign a commitment statement:

"I commit to focusing my primary change energy on _____ for the next 90 days. I understand this means saying no to other improvements during this time. I believe this choice will create the foundation for all other changes I want to make. I am ready to begin."

Signature: _____ Date: _____

Step 11: The Announcement Tell someone important to you about your ONE choice:

- Who will you tell about this decision?

- How will you ask for their support?

- What accountability do you want from them?

The goal isn't to choose perfectly - it's to choose consciously and commit fully to your choice.

Tomorrow, you'll dive deep into understanding your chosen area completely so you can develop an effective approach. But today, focus on making the decision that will shape your next season of growth.

This is where transformation begins: not with perfect plans or ideal circumstances, but with the courage to choose ONE thing and commit to it completely.

Your ONE choice is your declaration that you're serious about change. Make it count.

TWENTY-TWO

Day 21: Deep Dive Into Your Focus

Understanding your chosen area completely

You've made the choice. You've committed to your ONE focus area for the next 90 days. Now comes the work that most people skip: truly understanding what you're trying to change before you start trying to change it.

Most transformation attempts fail not because people choose the wrong focus, but because they don't understand their chosen area deeply enough to create an effective approach. They jump straight to tactics and strategies without first understanding the root causes, patterns, and systems that create their current reality.

Today is about becoming an expert on your chosen focus area so you can design changes that actually work with your life instead of against it.

***

The Root Cause Investigation

Your current situation in this area isn't random. It's the result of specific patterns, habits, systems, and choices that have been operating over time - many of them unconsciously.

Before you can change the results, you need to understand what's creating them.

If your focus is energy management, what specific habits, schedules, and choices are creating your current energy patterns?

If your focus is authentic communication, what fears, beliefs, and past experiences are keeping you from being genuine in difficult conversations?

If your focus is time boundaries, what internal and external pressures are causing you to consistently over-commit?

The deeper you understand the root causes, the more effective your change strategy will be.

***

The Pattern Recognition Process

Look for recurring patterns in your chosen area:

- When does the problem show up most consistently?

- What triggers typically precede the behavior you want to change?

- What environments or relationships make the issue better or worse?

- What time of day, week, or season does this challenge peak?

- What emotions or mental states are connected to this area?

These patterns aren't obstacles - they're data that will help you design targeted interventions.

***

The System Analysis

Your current reality in this area is supported by systems - both internal systems (thoughts, habits, beliefs) and external systems (environment, schedule, relationships).

Internal systems that might be maintaining your current patterns:

- Automatic thoughts or beliefs

- Emotional patterns and triggers

- Habits and routines

- Skills or knowledge gaps

- Identity or role expectations

External systems that might be reinforcing current patterns:

- Physical environment and spaces

- Schedule and time allocation

- Relationship dynamics and expectations

- Work culture and demands

- Technology and tool usage

Understanding these systems helps you identify which ones need to change to support your new direction.

***

The Success and Failure Analysis

You've probably tried to improve this area before. Instead of ignoring past attempts, analyze them for insights:

Previous Success Analysis:

- When have you been successful in this area, even temporarily?

- What conditions supported those successes?

- What was different about your approach, mindset, or circumstances?

- What made those improvements stick or not stick?

Previous Failure Analysis:

- What strategies have you tried that didn't work?

- Where did those attempts break down?

- What obstacles consistently derailed your progress?

- What assumptions about change might have been incorrect?

This analysis prevents you from repeating failed approaches and helps you identify elements that worked that you can build on.

***

The Stakeholder Impact Assessment

Your change in this area will affect other people in your life. Understanding these impacts helps you anticipate resistance and build support:

- Who benefits from your current patterns in this area?

- Who might resist changes you make?

- Who would be most supportive of your improvement?

- How will changes affect your family, work relationships, or friendships?

- What conversations do you need to have to prepare others for your changes?

This isn't about getting permission to change, but about understanding the relational dynamics that could support or undermine your progress.

***

The Resource and Constraint Audit

Be realistic about what you have to work with:

Available Resources:

- How much time can you realistically dedicate to this change?

- What financial resources are available if needed?

- Who could provide support, accountability, or expertise?

- What tools, systems, or knowledge do you already have?

- What strengths can you leverage to make change easier?

Real Constraints:

- What legitimate limitations do you need to work within?

- What responsibilities can't be adjusted during this change process?

- What seasonal or temporary factors might affect your approach?

- What health, financial, or relationship constraints are genuinely limiting?

Understanding your real resources and constraints helps you design a change approach that's sustainable within your actual life.

***

Your Daily Challenge: Complete Focus Area Analysis

Today, you're going to become an expert on your chosen focus area so you can design an effective transformation approach.

Step 1: Focus Area Definition Clearly define your chosen focus:

- What exactly are you trying to change or improve?

- How will you know when you've made progress?

- What would success look like in this area?

Step 2: Current State Deep Dive Analyze your current reality in detail:

- How does this area currently function in your life?

- What are the specific behaviors, patterns, or results you want to change?

- When is this area at its worst? When is it at its best?

- How does this area affect other parts of your life?

Step 3: Root Cause Investigation Dig into what's creating your current patterns:

- What habits, choices, or systems are maintaining the current state?

- What beliefs or thoughts consistently show up in this area?

- What fears or concerns might be influencing your behavior?

- What past experiences shaped your current approach?

Step 4: Pattern Mapping Identify the recurring patterns:

- What triggers typically precede the behaviors you want to change?

- What environments, relationships, or circumstances make this area better or worse?

- What time patterns exist (daily, weekly, seasonal)?

- What emotional or energy patterns are connected to this area?

Step 5: System Analysis Map the systems that support your current reality:

Internal Systems:

- What automatic thoughts or beliefs operate in this area?

- What habits or routines are connected to this focus?

- What skills or knowledge might be missing?

- How does your identity or self-concept affect this area?

External Systems:

- How does your environment support or hinder progress?

- What schedule or time factors influence this area?

- How do relationships and social dynamics affect this?

- What tools, technology, or resources are currently involved?

Step 6: Historical Analysis Learn from your past attempts:

Previous Successes:

- When have you made progress in this area before?

- What conditions or approaches supported those successes?

- What made some improvements stick while others faded?

Previous Challenges:

- What strategies have you tried that didn't work?

- Where did past attempts typically break down?

- What obstacles have consistently derailed progress?

Step 7: Stakeholder Impact Assessment Consider how your changes will affect others:

- Who in your life is affected by your current patterns in this area?

- Who might resist changes you make? Who would be supportive?

- What conversations do you need to have to prepare others?

- How can you minimize negative impacts on relationships while still making necessary changes?

Step 8: Resource and Constraint Audit

Available Resources:

- Time: How much can you realistically dedicate to this change?

- Support: Who could provide accountability, advice, or assistance?

- Knowledge: What do you already know? What do you need to learn?

- Tools: What systems, apps, or resources could help?

- Strengths: What existing abilities can you leverage?

Real Constraints:

- What genuinely can't be changed during this 90-day focus?

- What seasonal, work, or family factors need to be considered?

- What health, financial, or relationship limitations are real?

Step 9: The Integration Assessment Consider how this focus connects to your larger vision:

- How does progress in this area support your overall integrated life vision?

- How does this focus align with your "I Am" statement and core values?

- What ripple effects do you expect in other areas of your life?

Step 10: The Insight Summary Write a comprehensive summary of what you've learned:

- What are the 3 most important insights about your current patterns?

- What are the 3 biggest obstacles you'll need to address?

- What are the 3 greatest advantages or resources you can leverage?

- Based on this analysis, what type of change approach is most likely to work?

Step 11: The Success Factors Identification Based on your analysis, identify what will be most critical for success:

- What conditions do you need to create to support this change?

- What habits or systems will need to be adjusted?

- What support or accountability will be most helpful?

- What could derail your progress, and how can you prepare for it?

The goal isn't to solve everything today. The goal is to understand your chosen area so completely that when you start designing your change approach tomorrow, you're working with accurate information rather than assumptions.

This deep dive work is what separates successful transformation from repeated failed attempts. You're not just trying harder - you're being smarter about what you're trying to change and why.

Tomorrow, we'll begin Week 4 by setting specific 30/60/90 day goals based on everything you've learned. But today, focus on becoming an expert on the area you've chosen to transform.

Because you can't change what you don't understand, and understanding is what transforms hope into strategy.

TWENTY-THREE

Day 22: The Next 90

Breaking down your vision into achievable milestones

You have a clear vision of your integrated life. You understand your current reality. You've chosen your ONE focus area and analyzed it completely. Now comes the bridge between vision and reality: setting specific, achievable goals that will move you steadily toward the life you want to create.

Most people set goals that are either too vague to be actionable or too ambitious to be sustainable. They create elaborate annual resolutions or distant dreams without building the stepping stones that make progress possible.

Today is about breaking down your transformation into manageable milestones that create momentum while building toward significant change.

***

The Progressive Milestone Strategy

Real transformation happens through progressive milestones, not dramatic leaps. Each milestone should be challenging enough to create growth but achievable enough to build confidence and momentum.

Think of your 90-day journey like climbing a mountain:

- 30 days: Base camp - establishing foundation habits and systems

- 60 days: Halfway point - deepening and expanding your progress

- 90 days: Summit - achieving significant transformation in your focus area

Each milestone builds on the previous one, creating compound progress that accelerates over time.

***

The Foundation-First Principle

Your 30-day goal should focus on establishing the foundation for change rather than achieving dramatic results. This is about creating the conditions that make sustainable progress possible.

If your focus is energy management, your 30-day goal might be establishing consistent sleep and morning routines, not completely transforming your energy levels.

If your focus is authentic communication, your 30-day goal might be having one honest conversation per week, not becoming completely transparent in all relationships.

If your focus is time boundaries, your 30-day goal might be saying no to one non-essential commitment per week, not perfectly managing your entire schedule.

Foundation goals feel less exciting because they're about systems rather than outcomes. But they're what make everything else possible.

***

The Momentum Building Design

Your 60-day goal should build on the foundation you've established in the first 30 days and expand your progress. This is where you start seeing more visible results from the systems you've built.

This milestone should feel like a natural progression from your 30-day achievement, not a completely different challenge. You're deepening and expanding what you've already started rather than starting something new.

***

The Integration Milestone

Your 90-day goal should demonstrate significant progress in your focus area while creating positive ripple effects in other areas of your life. This is where integration becomes visible - where improvement in your chosen area naturally supports improvement everywhere else.

By day 90, you should be able to look back and see not just progress in your focus area, but evidence that this progress has made you more effective, present, and authentic across all areas of your life.

***

The SMART-ER Goal Framework

Each milestone should be SMART-ER:

- **Specific:** Clear about exactly what you want to achieve

- **Measurable:** You can objectively assess progress and completion

- **Achievable:** Realistic given your current reality and constraints

- **Relevant:** Directly connected to your focus area and larger vision

- **Time-bound:** Has a clear deadline

- **Exciting:** Motivates you to take action

- **Reviewed:** You have a system for tracking progress and making adjustments

***

The Energy and Capacity Reality Check

Your goals need to account for your actual energy and capacity, not your ideal energy and capacity.

Consider your current life demands:

- What other responsibilities require your attention during this 90-day period?

- What seasonal factors (work cycles, family commitments, health considerations) might affect your capacity?

- How much time and energy can you realistically dedicate to this focus area?

- What support systems do you have or need to create?

Realistic goals that account for your actual capacity are far more effective than ambitious goals that ignore your real constraints.

**

The Habit vs. Outcome Balance

Each milestone should include both habit goals (what you'll do consistently) and outcome goals (what results you'll achieve).

Habit goals are within your complete control and create the foundation for long-term success. Outcome goals provide motivation and direction but may be influenced by factors beyond your control.

Example for energy management focus:

- 30-day habit goal: Sleep 7+ hours and exercise 20 minutes daily

- 30-day outcome goal: Feel energized rather than exhausted most afternoons

***

Your Daily Challenge: Strategic Milestone Planning

Today, you're going to create your 30/60/90 day roadmap based on everything you've learned about yourself and your focus area.

Step 1: Focus Area Review Remind yourself of your chosen focus and why it matters:

- What is your ONE focus area for the next 90 days?

- Why did you choose this area as your highest priority?

- What would success look like in this area?

- How will progress here create ripple effects in other areas?

Step 2: Current Reality Baseline Establish your starting point:

- Where are you currently in this focus area (be specific)?

- What are you currently doing or not doing that creates your current reality?

- What would need to change to move from where you are to where you want to be?

Step 3: 90-Day Vision Clarification Get clear on your ultimate destination for this focus period:

- What would significant progress in this area look like after 90 days?

- How would you be thinking, feeling, and acting differently?

- What evidence would you have that real change has occurred?

- How would others notice the change in you?

Step 4: Milestone Breakdown Strategy Plan your progressive approach:

30-Day Foundation Milestone:

- What foundational habits or systems need to be established first?

- What would represent solid progress toward your 90-day vision?

- What would you need to accomplish to feel confident about continuing?

60-Day Expansion Milestone:

- How would you build on your 30-day foundation?

- What would represent significant momentum toward your 90-day vision?

- What deeper or more challenging aspects would you be ready to tackle?

90-Day Integration Milestone:

- What would represent substantial transformation in your focus area?

- How would this progress naturally support other areas of your life?

- What would you be capable of that you're not capable of now?

Step 5: SMART-ER Goal Crafting

30-Day Goal:

- Specific: What exactly will you achieve or establish?

- Measurable: How will you track progress and know when you've succeeded?

- Achievable: Is this realistic given your current capacity and constraints?

- Relevant: How does this directly support your focus area?

- Time-bound: What is your specific deadline?

- Exciting: Does this motivate you to take action?

- Reviewed: How will you track progress and adjust if needed?

60-Day Goal: [Repeat SMART-ER framework]

90-Day Goal: [Repeat SMART-ER framework]

Step 6: Habit and Outcome Balance For each milestone, identify both:

30-Day Goals:

- Habit Goal (what you'll do consistently): _____

- Outcome Goal (what result you'll achieve):
  _____

60-Day Goals:

- Habit Goal:
  _____

- Outcome Goal:
  _____

90-Day Goals:

- Habit Goal:
  _____

- Outcome Goal:
  _____

Step 7: Resource and Support Planning For each milestone, identify:

- What resources (time, tools, knowledge) will you need?

- What support or accountability would be helpful?

- What obstacles might derail progress and how will you address them?

- What adjustments to your current life might be necessary?

Step 8: Integration Assessment For each milestone, consider:

- How will progress in your focus area affect your work life?

- How will it affect your family relationships?

- How will it affect your energy and well-being?

- How will it support your overall integrated life vision?

Step 9: The Reality Check Review all three milestones and ask:

- Do these goals build logically on each other?

- Are you trying to change too much too quickly?

- Do these timelines account for your actual capacity?

- Would achieving these milestones represent significant progress?

- Are you excited about working toward these goals?

Step 10: The Commitment Declaration Write and sign your commitment to these milestones:

"I commit to achieving the following milestones in my focus area of _____:

30 days: _____

60 days: _____

90 days: _____

I understand these goals will require consistent effort and may need adjustment as I learn and grow. I am committed to the process, not just the outcomes."

Signature: _____ Date: _____

Step 11: Next Step Identification Based on your 30-day goal, identify:

- What is the very first action you need to take?

- When will you take this action?

- What needs to be in place for you to begin?

The goal isn't to create perfect predictions of the future. The goal is to create clear direction and achievable milestones that will guide your daily choices and actions.

Tomorrow, you'll break these milestones down into weekly action steps. But today, focus on creating the roadmap that will turn your vision into reality.

Because vision without milestones is just a dream. But milestones without vision are just tasks. Together, they create the bridge between where you are and where you want to be.

TWENTY-FOUR

Day 23: Weekly Action Steps

The specific things you'll do each week

You have your 30/60/90 day milestones. You know where you're headed and what success looks like at each stage. Now comes the part that determines whether your goals become reality or remain good intentions: breaking them down into specific weekly actions.

This is where most transformation efforts fail. People set inspiring goals but never create the detailed action plans that make achievement possible. They know what they want to accomplish but not exactly how they'll accomplish it.

Weekly action steps are the bridge between your milestones and your daily reality. They transform abstract goals into concrete behaviors you can actually implement.

***

The Weekly Planning Advantage

Weekly planning is the sweet spot for sustainable change. Daily planning can feel overwhelming and micromanaged. Monthly planning often lacks the specificity needed to drive consistent action.

But weekly planning gives you enough detail to know exactly what to do while maintaining enough flexibility to adapt to real life as it happens.

A week is long enough to make meaningful progress but short enough to maintain focus. It's long enough to establish patterns but short enough to course-correct quickly if something isn't working.

***

The System vs. Goal Integration

Your weekly action steps should include both goal-directed activities (specific things you do to achieve your milestones) and system-building activities (habits and routines that support long-term success).

Goal-directed activities create immediate progress toward your milestones. System-building activities create the foundation for sustainable change beyond your 90-day focus period.

The most effective weekly plans balance both types of activities.

***

The Minimum Effective Dose Principle

Each week should include the minimum effective dose of action - the smallest amount of activity that will create meaningful progress without overwhelming your capacity.

This isn't about doing the least possible. It's about identifying the specific actions that will have the biggest impact and focusing your energy there rather than spreading it across too many activities.

Three focused actions per week that you complete consistently will create more progress than ten scattered actions that you do sporadically.

***

The Context and Constraint Integration

Your weekly action steps need to account for the realities of your actual life, not some idealized version of your schedule.

Consider your weekly rhythms:

- What days tend to be most demanding at work?

- When do you have the most energy and focus?

- What family or personal commitments are consistent each week?

- When are you most likely to have uninterrupted time?

Design your action steps to work with your natural rhythms rather than against them.

***

The Progress Measurement Strategy

Each weekly action should be measurable so you can objectively assess whether you're making progress or need to adjust your approach.

Vague actions like "be more authentic" or "manage energy better" don't provide clear direction or measurable progress.

Specific actions like "have one honest conversation about a difficult topic" or "maintain 7+ hours of sleep on weeknights" give you clear targets and measurable outcomes.

***

The Flexibility Framework

Your weekly action steps should be specific enough to drive behavior but flexible enough to adapt to unexpected circumstances.

Build in options and alternatives so that disruptions don't derail your entire week. If your planned action becomes impossible, what's the backup plan that keeps you moving forward?

***

Your Daily Challenge: Weekly Action Architecture

Today, you're going to create the specific weekly action plan that will turn your milestones into reality.

Step 1: Milestone Review Remind yourself of your three milestones:

- 30-day goal:
  _____

- 60-day goal:
  _____

- 90-day goal:
  _____

Step 2: 30-Day Milestone Breakdown Focus first on your 30-day foundation milestone. Break it down into what needs to happen each week:

Week 1 (Days 1-7):

- What needs to be established or initiated?
- What foundational habits need to begin?
- What systems need to be set up?

Week 2 (Days 8-14):

- How will you build on Week 1's foundation?
- What habits need to be strengthened or expanded?
- What new elements can be added?

Week 3 (Days 15-21):

- How will you deepen your practice?

- What adjustments might be needed based on early results?

- What challenges are you likely to face and how will you address them?

Week 4 (Days 22-30):

- How will you consolidate your progress?

- What would need to be true to achieve your 30-day milestone?

- How will you prepare for expanding toward your 60-day goal?

Step 3: Specific Action Identification For each of the first four weeks, identify 2-3 specific actions you'll take:

Week 1 Actions:

1.

2.

Week 2 Actions:

1.

2.

3.

Week 3 Actions:

1.

2.

3.

Week 4 Actions:

1.

2.

3.

Step 4: Action Specification For each action, make it SMARTER:

Example format: *Action:* "Have one authentic conversation about a challenging topic" *Specific:* "Initiate a conversation with [person] about [specific topic] that I've been avoiding" *Measurable:* "Complete one genuine conversation where I express my actual thoughts/feelings" *Achievable:* "Choose a topic that's important but not catastrophic if handled imperfectly" *Relevant:* "Directly practices authentic communication in relationships" *Time-bound:* "By end of the week" *Exciting:* "Will reduce internal tension and improve relationship authenticity" *Reviewed:* "Assess conversation quality and plan next week's conversation"

Step 5: Context Integration For each weekly action, identify:

- When during the week will you do this? (specific day/time if possible)

- What conditions need to be in place for success?

- What might interfere with this action and how will you handle it?

- What preparation is needed before taking this action?

Step 6: System Building Integration For each week, identify one system-building activity that supports long-term success:

Week 1 System: _____

How this supports long-term change: _____

Week 2 System: _____

How this supports long-term change: _____

Week 3 System: _____

How this supports long-term change: _____

Week 4 System: _____

How this supports long-term change: _____

Step 7: Progress Measurement Design For each weekly action, define how you'll measure progress:

- What will successful completion look like?

- How will you track whether you did what you planned?

- What qualitative assessment will you make (how did it feel, what did you learn)?

- What adjustments might be needed based on results?

Step 8: Flexibility Planning For each weekly action, create a backup plan:

- If circumstances prevent your planned action, what's the minimum viable alternative?

Day 23: Weekly Action Steps

- How will you maintain momentum if your week gets disrupted?

- What counts as progress even if you can't complete the full action?

Step 9: Integration Assessment For each week's actions, consider:

- How do these actions support your overall integrated life vision?

- How will completing these actions affect other areas of your life?

- What ripple effects do you expect from this week's focus?

Step 10: Energy and Capacity Check Review your four-week plan:

- Is this amount of weekly activity sustainable given your other commitments?

- Are you trying to do too much or too little each week?

- Do these actions work with your natural energy patterns and weekly rhythms?

- What adjustments would make this plan more realistic?

Step 11: The Weekly Planning System Design your ongoing weekly planning process:

- When each week will you review progress and plan the following week?

- How will you adjust actions based on what you learn?

- What will you do if you fall behind or need to modify your approach?

- How will you maintain momentum when motivation decreases?

Step 12: Week 1 Preparation Focus on preparing for immediate action:

- What is your very first action for Week 1?

- What needs to be in place before you can begin?

- When exactly will you take this first action?

- How will you track and assess your progress?

Step 13: The Action Commitment Write and sign your commitment to taking weekly action:

"I commit to taking specific weekly actions toward my 30-day milestone of _____. I understand that consistent weekly progress is more important than perfect execution. I will review and adjust my approach based on what I learn, while maintaining commitment to forward movement."

Signature: _____ Date: _____

The goal isn't to create a perfect plan that never needs adjustment. The goal is to create specific enough direction that you know exactly what to do each week while maintaining enough flexibility to adapt as you learn and grow.

Tomorrow, you'll design your accountability system to help you stay on track when motivation fades. But today, focus on creating the detailed roadmap that transforms your milestones into weekly reality.

Because goals without actions are just wishes. But actions without goals are just busy work. Together, they create the path from where you are to where you want to be.

TWENTY-FIVE

Day 24: Staying On Track

How you'll stay on track when motivation fades

You have your goals. You have your weekly action plan. You're ready to begin making real changes in your focus area. But here's what every person who's ever tried to transform their life discovers: motivation is unreliable.

The excitement you feel right now about your transformation journey will fade. The clarity you have about your goals will get cloudy when life gets complicated. The commitment you feel to your action plan will waver when those actions become inconvenient or uncomfortable.

This isn't a character flaw. This is human nature. And successful people account for it by building accountability systems that keep them moving forward when internal motivation isn't enough.

***

The Motivation Myth

Most people believe that successful change requires constant motivation. They think that if they just want it badly enough, they'll naturally do what needs to be done.

But motivation is an emotion, and emotions are temporary. You can't base lasting change on something as unreliable as how you feel in the moment.

Successful transformation is built on systems, not feelings. It's built on external accountability structures that keep you moving forward regardless of your internal motivation level.

***

The Internal vs. External Accountability Balance

There are two types of accountability: internal and external. You need both.

Internal accountability is your relationship with yourself - your ability to keep commitments you make to yourself even when no one else is watching.

External accountability involves other people - creating relationships and structures where others are aware of your commitments and will notice if you don't follow through.

Most people rely too heavily on internal accountability and wonder why they keep letting themselves down. But internal accountability is the weakest form of accountability because it's the easiest to rationalize away.

External accountability works because it leverages social pressure and relationship dynamics to reinforce your commitments.

***

The Accountability Spectrum

Not all accountability is created equal. Different types of accountability provide different levels of support and pressure:

Announcement Accountability: Telling others about your goals *Strength:* Easy to implement, creates initial social pressure *Weakness:* People forget, no ongoing support, easy to make excuses

Progress Reporting: Regularly updating others on your progress *Strength:* Creates ongoing awareness, maintains visibility *Weakness:* Can become performative, may lack meaningful feedback

Partnership Accountability: Working with someone who has similar goals *Strength:* Mutual support, shared understanding of challenges *Weakness:* Can enable each other's excuses, may lack outside perspective

Coach/Mentor Accountability: Working with someone experienced in your area of change *Strength:* Expert guidance, objective perspective, proven strategies *Weakness:* Requires investment, may feel like additional pressure

Consequence Accountability: Creating real stakes for not following through *Strength:* Strong motivation to avoid negative outcomes *Weakness:* Can feel punitive, may create resistance

The most effective accountability systems combine multiple levels rather than relying on just one approach.

***

The Feedback Loop Design

Good accountability isn't just about tracking whether you did what you said you'd do. It's about creating feedback loops that help you learn and adjust your approach.

Your accountability system should help you:

- Recognize patterns in what works and what doesn't
- Identify obstacles before they derail your progress
- Celebrate successes to build momentum
- Make adjustments to your plan based on real experience
- Stay connected to your deeper reasons for change

***

The Shame vs. Support Balance

Accountability can quickly become shame-based if not designed thoughtfully. Shame-based accountability creates guilt about failure rather than support for success.

Supportive accountability focuses on:

- Learning from setbacks rather than punishing them
- Adjusting strategies rather than questioning commitment
- Celebrating progress rather than only noting failures

- Understanding obstacles rather than making excuses

- Maintaining long-term perspective rather than getting stuck on short-term lapses

***

Your Daily Challenge: Accountability Architecture

Today, you're going to design a comprehensive accountability system that will support your success throughout your 90-day transformation journey.

Step 1: Accountability Assessment Reflect on your past change attempts:

- When you've successfully made changes before, what accountability helped?

- When you've failed to maintain changes, what accountability was missing?

- Do you tend to be harder on yourself or easier on yourself when you miss commitments?

- What type of external support is most motivating for you?

- What type of accountability do you tend to resist or avoid?

Step 2: Internal Accountability Design Create your relationship with yourself around this change:

Self-Commitment Contract: Write a contract with yourself that includes:

- Your commitment to your 90-day focus and 30/60/90 milestones

- What you'll do when you face setbacks or lose motivation

- How you'll talk to yourself when things get difficult

- What you'll remember about why this change matters to you

Progress Tracking System: Design how you'll monitor your own progress:

- How will you track daily/weekly actions?

- What questions will you ask yourself weekly to assess progress?

- How will you celebrate small wins along the way?

- When will you do weekly/monthly reviews of your progress?

Step 3: External Accountability Selection Choose the external accountability that will work best for your personality and situation:

Option 1: Accountability Partner

- Who in your life could serve as an accountability partner?

- What would you want them to do to support your success?

- How often would you check in with them?

- What would you offer them in return?

Option 2: Mentor/Coach Relationship

- Do you know someone with experience in your focus area who could mentor you?

- Would investing in professional coaching be valuable for this change?

- What specific guidance would you want from a mentor?

Option 3: Group Accountability

- Is there a group (online or offline) focused on your type of change?

- Could you form a small group with others working on similar goals?

- What would make group accountability helpful rather than just social?

Option 4: Public Accountability

- Would sharing your journey publicly (social media, blog, etc.) be motivating?

- What level of public sharing feels supportive rather than performative?

- How would you handle public accountability without making it about image management?

Step 4: Consequence Design Create meaningful but not punitive consequences:

Positive Consequences (rewards for following through):

- What will you do to celebrate weekly progress?

- What reward will you give yourself for achieving your 30-day milestone?

- How will you acknowledge your effort regardless of perfect outcomes?

Natural Consequences (automatic results of not following through):

- What naturally happens when you don't take your planned actions?

- How can you make these natural consequences more visible?

- What would you lose by not following through that you don't want to lose?

Step 5: Support System Activation Identify the support you need beyond accountability:

Practical Support:

- What practical help would make your actions easier to complete?

- Who could provide childcare, schedule flexibility, or other logistics support?

- What tools, resources, or information would be helpful?

Emotional Support:

- Who do you want to know about this journey who can provide encouragement?

- What type of emotional support is most helpful when you're struggling?

- How will you ask for support when you need it?

Step 6: Feedback Loop Creation Design how you'll learn and adjust:

Weekly Review Questions:

- What actions did I complete this week?

- What actions did I miss and why?

- What did I learn about what works/doesn't work for me?

- What adjustments do I need to make for next week?

- How am I feeling about my progress and the process?

Monthly Assessment Questions:

- Am I on track for my milestones?

- What patterns am I noticing in my successes and challenges?

- What about my approach needs to be adjusted?

- How is this change affecting other areas of my life?

- What additional support or resources would be helpful?

Step 7: Accountability Schedule Create specific timing for your accountability:

Daily: What will you do each day to maintain internal accountability? **Weekly:** When and how will you review progress and connect with external accountability? **Monthly:** When will you do deeper assessment and plan adjustments?

Step 8: Resistance Planning Prepare for when you don't want accountability:

- When are you most likely to avoid accountability?

- What stories will you tell yourself to justify skipping check-ins?

- How will you handle the desire to quit when things get difficult?

- What will you do when external accountability feels like pressure rather than support?

Step 9: The Accountability Launch Prepare to activate your system:

Internal Launch:

- When will you begin tracking your progress?

- How will you set up your tracking system?

- When will you do your first weekly review?

External Launch:

- Who will you contact to set up external accountability?

- What conversation do you need to have to explain what you need?

- When will you have this conversation?

Step 10: The Accountability Commitment Write and sign your commitment to using accountability:

"I commit to maintaining both internal and external accountability throughout my 90-day transformation journey. I understand that motivation will fade and that accountability systems will keep me moving forward when feelings aren't enough. I will use setbacks as learning opportunities rather than reasons to quit."

My Internal Accountability Plan:
_____

My External Accountability Plan:
_____

My Review Schedule:
_____

Signature: _____ Date: _____

The goal isn't to create perfect accountability that prevents all lapses. The goal is to create support systems that help you get back on track quickly when you inevitably face challenges.

Tomorrow, you'll prepare for obstacles by planning how you'll handle the predictable challenges that could derail your progress. But today, focus on building the accountability architecture that will support your success.

Because motivation gets you started, but accountability keeps you going. And staying on track when it's hard is what separates temporary change from lasting transformation.

TWENTY-SIX

Day 25: When It Goes Wrong

What could go wrong and how you'll handle it

You have your goals, your action plan, and your accountability system. You're ready to begin your transformation journey. But here's what successful people know that dreamers don't: obstacles aren't interruptions to your plan - they are part of your plan.

Every transformation journey includes predictable challenges. Your motivation will wane. Life will get complicated. Old patterns will resist change. Unexpected events will disrupt your routine.

Most people treat these obstacles as reasons to quit or evidence that their plan isn't working. But successful people anticipate obstacles and develop strategies to work through them before they occur.

Today is about obstacle-proofing your transformation by planning for what could go wrong so you can handle it when it does.

***

The Obstacle Inevitability Principle

Obstacles aren't signs of failure - they're signs that you're attempting something meaningful. If your change journey doesn't include challenges, you're probably not pushing yourself hard enough to create real transformation.

The goal isn't to eliminate all obstacles. The goal is to expect them, prepare for them, and develop the resilience to work through them without abandoning your larger vision.

***

The Predictable Obstacle Categories

Most transformation obstacles fall into predictable categories. By identifying which categories are most likely to affect you, you can prepare specific strategies for each.

Time and Schedule Obstacles:

- Competing priorities that demand your attention
- Unexpected commitments or crises
- Seasonal changes in your schedule or demands
- Travel, illness, or family obligations

Energy and Motivation Obstacles:

- The initial excitement wearing off
- Feeling overwhelmed by the effort required
- Burnout from trying to change too much too quickly
- Lack of visible progress creating discouragement

Social and Relationship Obstacles:

- Family or friends who resist your changes
- Workplace culture that doesn't support your new patterns
- Social situations that tempt you back to old behaviors

- Lack of understanding or support from important people

Internal and Psychological Obstacles:

- Fear of failure or success

- Perfectionism that makes you quit when you're not perfect

- Old identity or self-talk that contradicts your new direction

- Imposter syndrome or feeling like you don't deserve success

External and Circumstantial Obstacles:

- Financial pressures that limit your options

- Health issues that affect your capacity

- Major life changes that disrupt your routine

- Environmental factors that make change more difficult

***

The Pre-Mortem Strategy

A pre-mortem is the opposite of a post-mortem. Instead of analyzing what went wrong after failure, you imagine potential failure scenarios in advance and develop prevention and response strategies.

For your transformation journey, this means:

- Identifying the most likely ways your plan could get derailed

- Developing specific strategies to prevent these derailments

- Creating response plans for when prevention isn't enough

- Building resilience systems that help you recover quickly from setbacks

***

The Minimum Viable Progress Concept

One of the most effective obstacle strategies is defining minimum viable progress - the smallest amount of forward movement that maintains momentum during difficult periods.

When obstacles make your full action plan impossible, what's the minimum you could do to stay connected to your change process?

If you can't complete your weekly actions, what could you do to maintain the habit pattern?

If you can't work toward your milestone for a week, what would prevent you from losing all progress?

Minimum viable progress keeps you in the game during challenging periods so you can return to full effort when circumstances improve.

***

The Obstacle Opportunity Reframe

Advanced obstacle planning goes beyond just surviving challenges - it looks for ways that obstacles can actually strengthen your transformation.

How could a schedule disruption teach you better prioritization skills?

How could resistance from others help you clarify your boundaries and values?

How could a motivation crash help you develop better systems and accountability?

How could unexpected changes help you become more adaptable and resilient?

This reframe doesn't minimize the difficulty of obstacles, but it helps you extract value from challenges rather than just enduring them.

***

Your Daily Challenge: Comprehensive Obstacle Preparation

Today, you're going to identify the most likely obstacles to your transformation and develop specific strategies to handle them.

Step 1: Personal Obstacle History Reflect on your past change attempts:

- What obstacles have derailed your progress in the past?

- What patterns do you notice in how and when you tend to give up?

- What external circumstances have made change difficult before?

- What internal patterns (thoughts, emotions, behaviors) have sabotaged previous efforts?

Step 2: Current Life Obstacle Assessment Consider your current circumstances:

- What competing priorities might interfere with your focus area?

- What relationships might resist or not support your changes?

- What seasonal or temporary factors might create challenges?

- What aspects of your current lifestyle might conflict with your new direction?

Step 3: Category-Specific Obstacle Identification

Time and Schedule Obstacles:

- What could disrupt your weekly action plan?

- When are you most likely to be too busy for your planned actions?

- What events or obligations might conflict with your change work?

Energy and Motivation Obstacles:

- When do you typically lose motivation in change processes?

- What discourages you most when trying to change?

- What would make you feel like quitting this transformation journey?

Social and Relationship Obstacles:

- Who might resist or not understand your changes?

- What social situations might tempt you back to old patterns?

- Where might you face pressure to abandon your new direction?

Internal and Psychological Obstacles:

- What fears might sabotage your progress?

- What negative self-talk might undermine your efforts?

- What perfectionist tendencies might cause you to quit?

External and Circumstantial Obstacles:

- What circumstances could make your planned actions difficult or impossible?

- What environmental factors might work against your goals?

- What practical constraints might limit your options?

Step 4: Likelihood and Impact Assessment For each obstacle you've identified, rate:

- Likelihood (1-10): How probable is this obstacle?

- Impact (1-10): How much would this obstacle disrupt your progress?

- Control (1-10): How much influence do you have over this obstacle?

Step 5: Top 5 Obstacle Selection Based on your assessment, identify your 5 most significant obstacles.

Obstacle: _____

Type: _____

Likelihood: ___ Impact: ___ Control: ___

Obstacle: _____

Type: _____

Likelihood: ___ Impact: ___ Control: ___

Obstacle: _____

Type: _____

Likelihood: ___ Impact: ___ Control: ___

Obstacle: _____

Type: _____

Likelihood: ___ Impact: ___ Control: ___

Obstacle: _____

Type: _____

Likelihood: ___ Impact: ___ Control: ___

Step 6: Prevention Strategy Development For each of your top 5 obstacles, develop prevention strategies:

Obstacle 1 Prevention:

- What could you do to make this obstacle less likely to occur?

- What changes to your plan or environment would reduce this risk?

- How could you prepare in advance to minimize this obstacle's impact?

[Repeat for obstacles 2-5]

Step 7: Response Strategy Creation For each obstacle, create a specific response plan:

Obstacle 1 Response:

- What will you do if this obstacle occurs despite prevention efforts?

- What's your minimum viable progress if this obstacle temporarily stops your full plan?

- How will you get back on track once this obstacle is resolved?

- Who could help you work through this challenge?

[Repeat for obstacles 2-5]

Step 8: Minimum Viable Progress Definition For different levels of disruption, define your minimum viable progress:

Minor Disruption (busy week but still functional): Minimum actions: _____

Major Disruption (significant life event or crisis): Minimum actions: _____

Complete Disruption (impossible to work on goals): Minimum connection:

_____

Step 9: Opportunity Reframe Development For each of your top obstacles, identify potential growth opportunities:

- How could working through this obstacle make you stronger?

- What skills or insights might you develop by overcoming this challenge?

- How could this obstacle actually serve your larger transformation?

Step 10: Recovery Protocol Design Create your standard process for getting back on track after obstacles:

The Obstacle Recovery Process:

1. Acknowledge what happened without judgment

2. Assess what you learned from the experience

3. Adjust your plan based on new information

4. Reconnect with your deeper motivation for change

5. Restart with minimum viable progress

6. Gradually return to full action plan

7. Strengthen systems to prevent similar future obstacles

Step 11: Support System Activation For each major obstacle, identify:

- Who could provide practical help if this obstacle occurs?

- Who could provide emotional support during this challenge?

- What resources or information would be helpful?

- How will you ask for help when you need it?

Step 12: The Obstacle Commitment Write and sign your commitment to working through obstacles:

"I commit to expecting and preparing for obstacles as a normal part of my transformation journey. I will not treat challenges as reasons to quit but as opportunities to develop resilience and refine my approach. When obstacles occur, I will use my prepared strategies rather than abandoning my goals."

My biggest anticipated obstacle:
_____

My prevention strategy: _____

My response plan:
_____

My minimum viable progress: _____

Signature: _____ Date: _____

The goal isn't to eliminate all obstacles or have perfect responses to every challenge. The goal is to normalize obstacles as part of the process and have thoughtful strategies ready so you don't have to figure out what to do in the middle of a crisis.

Tomorrow, you'll define how you'll measure progress beyond just achievement of goals. But today, focus on obstacle-proofing your transformation so challenges become stepping stones rather than roadblocks.

Because expecting obstacles doesn't mean expecting failure. It means expecting to work through challenges successfully because you've prepared for them in advance.

TWENTY-SEVEN

Day 26: What Even Is Success

How you'll know you're making progress

You've built a comprehensive transformation plan. You have goals, actions, accountability, and obstacle strategies. Now comes a crucial question that most people never ask: How will you actually know if it's working?

Most transformation attempts fail not because people don't make progress, but because they don't recognize the progress they're making. They're so focused on the dramatic end result that they miss the subtle signs of positive change happening along the way.

Without clear success metrics, you'll either quit too early because you can't see progress, or you'll continue ineffective strategies too long because you're not measuring the right things.

Today is about defining how you'll measure success so you can celebrate progress, course-correct when needed, and maintain motivation throughout your journey.

***

The Multi-Dimensional Success Model

Real transformation happens across multiple dimensions, not just in the obvious, measurable outcomes people typically track.

Outcome Metrics: The end results you're trying to achieve
Process Metrics: How consistently you're taking the actions that lead to outcomes **Experience Metrics:** How the journey feels and what you're learning **Integration Metrics:** How changes in your focus area affect other areas of your life

Most people only track outcome metrics, which creates several problems:

- Outcomes are often delayed, so you don't see progress for weeks or months
- Outcomes can be influenced by factors outside your control

- Focusing only on outcomes ignores the process improvements that predict long-term success

A comprehensive success measurement system tracks all four dimensions.

***

The Leading vs. Lagging Indicator Balance

Lagging indicators tell you what has already happened - the results you've achieved. **Leading indicators** predict what will happen - the behaviors and processes that create results.

If your goal is better energy management, a lagging indicator might be "feel energized most afternoons." A leading indicator might be "sleep 7+ hours and exercise daily."

If your goal is authentic communication, a lagging indicator might be "improved relationship satisfaction." A leading indicator might be "have one honest conversation per week."

Leading indicators are more actionable because they're completely within your control. Lagging indicators provide motivation and confirm that your leading indicators are working.

The best measurement systems track both types of indicators.

The Quantitative vs. Qualitative Balance

Some aspects of transformation can be measured numerically (hours of sleep, number of difficult conversations, days of consistent action). Other aspects are better assessed qualitatively (how authentic you feel, energy levels, relationship satisfaction).

Both types of measurement are valuable:

- Quantitative metrics provide objective data and clear progress tracking

- Qualitative metrics capture the experience and meaning of change

Don't try to quantify everything. Some of the most important aspects of transformation are subjective and are better captured through reflection questions than numerical scores.

***

The Comparison Trap Avoidance

Your success metrics should measure your progress against your own baseline, not against other people's results or some external standard.

The question isn't "Am I as good as [someone else]?" The question is "Am I better than I was [time period] ago?"

Personal transformation is inherently individual. Your starting point, your challenges, your circumstances, and your natural pace of change are unique to you.

***

The Progress vs. Perfection Distinction

Your metrics should measure progress, not perfection.

Progress metrics ask: "Am I moving in the right direction?" Perfection metrics ask: "Am I doing this flawlessly?"

Progress metrics are motivating because they acknowledge improvement. Perfection metrics are discouraging because they focus on gaps and failures.

Design your measurement system to celebrate progress while honestly assessing areas that need adjustment.

***

Your Daily Challenge: Comprehensive Success Measurement Design

Today, you're going to create a multi-dimensional measurement system that will help you recognize progress and stay motivated throughout your transformation journey.

Step 1: Baseline Establishment Define your current starting point in detail:

Focus Area Baseline:

- Where are you right now in your chosen focus area?

- What specific behaviors, patterns, or results characterize your current state?

- How do you currently feel about this area of your life?

- How does this area currently affect other parts of your life?

Integration Baseline:

- How authentic do you feel across different areas of your life right now?

- How much internal conflict do you experience between different roles/contexts?

- How energized vs. drained do you feel by your current lifestyle?

Step 2: Outcome Metrics Definition Define the end results you're working toward:

30-Day Outcome Metrics:

- What specific results would indicate success at your 30-day milestone?

- How will you measure whether you've achieved your 30-day goal?

- What would be different about your life/experience if you reach this milestone?

60-Day Outcome Metrics:

- What results would indicate success at your 60-day milestone?

- How will these results build on your 30-day achievements?

90-Day Outcome Metrics:

- What results would represent significant transformation in your focus area?

- How will you know if you've successfully established sustainable change?

Step 3: Process Metrics Development Define the behaviors and actions that predict your outcome success:

Daily Process Metrics:

- What daily actions most directly contribute to your goals?

- How will you track whether you're taking these actions consistently?

- What percentage of daily actions completed indicates good progress?

Weekly Process Metrics:

- What weekly patterns or achievements indicate you're on track?

- How will you measure the quality of your weekly actions, not just completion?

- What weekly consistency rate would represent success?

Step 4: Experience Metrics Creation Define how you'll assess the qualitative aspects of your journey:

Weekly Experience Questions:

- How authentic did I feel in my focus area this week?

- What did I learn about myself or my change process?

- How challenged vs. overwhelmed did I feel?

- What unexpected insights or growth did I experience?

Monthly Experience Assessment:

- How is this change affecting my overall life satisfaction?

- What internal shifts am I noticing beyond the external changes?

- How is my relationship with change and growth evolving?

Step 5: Integration Metrics Design Define how you'll measure the ripple effects of your focused change:

Integration Indicators:

- How is progress in your focus area affecting your work performance?

- How is it affecting your family relationships and presence?

- How is it affecting your energy and well-being?

- How is it affecting your confidence and sense of authenticity?

Integration Questions:

- Am I becoming more of the same person across different contexts?

- Are the changes in my focus area making other areas of life easier or harder?

- How is this transformation supporting my overall integrated life vision?

Step 6: Leading Indicator Identification Identify the predictive behaviors you can control:

Daily Leading Indicators:

- What daily actions most reliably predict weekly success?

- Which habits, if maintained consistently, create the foundation for your goals?

Weekly Leading Indicators:

- What weekly patterns most reliably predict monthly progress?

- Which weekly achievements indicate you're building sustainable change?

Step 7: Measurement Schedule Design Create your tracking and assessment schedule:

Daily Tracking:

- What will you track daily? (Keep this simple - 1-3 metrics maximum)

- When during the day will you do this tracking?

- What tool/method will you use for daily tracking?

Weekly Assessment:

- When each week will you do your comprehensive progress review?

- What questions will you ask yourself weekly?

- How long will this weekly assessment take?

Monthly Evaluation:

- When each month will you do your deeper progress evaluation?

- What metrics will you analyze for trends and patterns?

- How will you use monthly data to adjust your approach?

Step 8: Progress Celebration System Define how you'll acknowledge and celebrate progress:

Weekly Progress Recognition:

- How will you acknowledge weekly progress, even if imperfect?

- What small celebrations will you do for weekly consistency?

Milestone Celebrations:

- How will you celebrate achieving your 30-day milestone?

- What meaningful (non-undermining) reward will you give yourself?

- How will you share your progress with others who support you?

Step 9: Course Correction Triggers Define when and how you'll adjust your approach:

Weekly Adjustment Indicators:

- What patterns would indicate you need to modify your weekly actions?

- How many weeks of missed targets would trigger a plan revision?

Monthly Strategy Review:

- What progress patterns would indicate your overall approach needs adjustment?

- How will you distinguish between normal obstacles and fundamental strategy problems?

Step 10: The Measurement Reality Check Review your entire measurement system:

- Is this tracking system simple enough that you'll actually use it?

- Are you measuring the things that matter most, not just what's easiest to measure?

- Does this system help you see progress rather than just failures?

- Will this measurement approach motivate you or create pressure?

Step 11: Measurement Tool Setup Choose your tracking methods:

- What app, journal, or system will you use for daily tracking?

- How will you store your weekly and monthly assessments?

- What format works best for your personality and lifestyle?

Step 12: The Measurement Commitment Write and sign your commitment to consistent measurement:

"I commit to tracking my progress using multiple types of metrics, not just final outcomes. I will use this data to celebrate progress, learn from setbacks, and adjust my approach when needed. I understand that measurement serves my growth, not my perfectionism."

My Daily Tracking: _____

My Weekly Assessment: _____

My Monthly Evaluation: _____

My Progress Celebration Plan: _____

Signature: _____ Date: _____

The goal isn't to create a perfect measurement system or track everything possible. The goal is to create visibility into your progress so you can stay motivated, learn continuously, and make data-driven adjustments to your approach.

Tomorrow, you'll create your action plan for the next 28 days to turn all this planning into immediate reality. But today, focus on designing measurement systems that will help you recognize and celebrate the progress you're about to make.

Because what gets measured gets achieved. But more importantly, what gets measured gets celebrated, and what gets celebrated gets repeated.

TWENTY-EIGHT

Day 27: Starting Tomorrow

The action plan that starts tomorrow

You've done the work. Twenty-six days of discovery, vision casting, reality assessment, and strategic planning. You know who you are, what you want to build, where you currently stand, and how you'll get there.

Now comes the moment that separates people who read about transformation from people who actually experience it: turning all this insight into immediate action.

Your next 28 days will determine whether this becomes another good idea you had or the beginning of lasting change in your life. This isn't about perfect execution - it's about consistent forward movement that builds momentum toward your integrated life vision.

***

The Implementation Imperative

Here's what happens to most people after they complete a planning process like this: they feel inspired by their insights, excited about their goals, and confident in their strategy. Then they go back to their regular life and gradually return to their old patterns.

The gap between planning and implementation is where most transformation dies.

Implementation requires shifting from thinking about change to actually changing. It requires moving from the safety of analysis to the vulnerability of action. It requires trading the comfort of preparation for the discomfort of practice.

Your next 28 days are your bridge between insight and transformation.

***

The First Month Foundation Strategy

Your first month of implementation has a specific purpose: establishing the foundation patterns that will support all future progress. This isn't about achieving dramatic results - it's about proving to yourself that sustainable change is possible.

The first month is about:

- Building consistency in small actions rather than perfection in big actions

- Creating new neural pathways through repetition

- Establishing accountability rhythms that support long-term change

- Learning what works in your real life versus what looked good on paper

- Building confidence through accumulated small wins

Think of this month as laying the groundwork for everything else you want to build.

***

The Minimum Viable Consistency Approach

Your success in the next 28 days won't be determined by how intensely you pursue change, but by how consistently you show up for it.

This means focusing on actions you can realistically maintain even during challenging weeks. It means choosing smaller changes that you complete regularly over larger changes that you do sporadically.

Consistency beats intensity when it comes to lasting transformation. The person who does something small every day for 28 days will create more sustainable change than the person who does something dramatic for three days and then stops.

***

The Learning Laboratory Mindset

Approach your next 28 days as a learning laboratory rather than a performance evaluation. You're not being graded on perfect execution - you're gathering data about what works for your unique situation.

Every day will teach you something:

- Which actions feel natural versus forced
- What obstacles show up and how to handle them

- How changes in your focus area affect other areas of your life

- What support systems are most helpful

- How to adjust your approach based on real experience

This experimental mindset removes the pressure of perfection and creates space for the trial and error that leads to sustainable solutions.

***

The Integration Momentum Principle

As you focus on your chosen area, pay attention to how progress there creates positive momentum in other areas of your life. This integration momentum is what transforms focused change into whole-life transformation.

When you improve your energy management, notice how it affects your patience with family members.

When you practice authentic communication, notice how it increases your confidence at work.

When you establish better boundaries, notice how it creates space for personal growth.

These ripple effects aren't automatic - they require conscious attention and intentional connection. But when you leverage them, focused change becomes integrated change.

***

Your Daily Challenge: Implementation Activation

Today, you're moving from planning to action by creating your specific 28-day implementation plan.

The Reality Bridge

First, connect your planning work to your upcoming reality. Look at your calendar for the next four weeks. What's happening in your life that might affect your change efforts? What busy periods, travel, family commitments, or work deadlines need to be factored into your approach?

This isn't about making excuses - it's about being realistic so your plan works with your actual life rather than against it.

The First Week Focus

Your first week is crucial because it sets the pattern for everything that follows. Choose one primary action you'll take consistently for seven days. This should be something directly related to your focus area that you can realistically complete even during busy or difficult days.

Make this action specific enough that you'll know whether you completed it, but flexible enough that you can adapt it to different circumstances. The goal is to establish the pattern of daily intentional action in your focus area.

The Week-by-Week Progression

Plan how you'll build on your first week's foundation:

Week two should deepen your initial action or add one complementary action. You're still establishing patterns, not dramatically expanding your efforts.

Week three can introduce more complexity or challenge as your foundational habits become more automatic.

Week four should focus on consistency and integration - maintaining your progress while paying attention to how it's affecting other areas of your life.

The Daily Rhythm Design

Decide when and how you'll engage with your change work each day. Most successful transformation happens when it's integrated into existing routines rather than added as separate obligations.

Consider your natural daily rhythms. When are you most energized and focused? When do you have the most control over your schedule? When would engaging with your focus area feel natural rather than forced?

Build your change actions into these optimal times rather than trying to force them into whatever time remains after everything else.

The Weekly Check-In System

Establish when and how you'll assess your progress each week. This isn't about judging yourself, but about learning what's working and what needs adjustment.

Choose a consistent day and time for your weekly review. Make it long enough to be thorough but short enough that you'll actually do it consistently. Fifteen to twenty minutes is usually sufficient.

Use this time to celebrate what went well, understand what was challenging, and make any necessary adjustments for the following week.

The Support Activation

Activate the accountability and support systems you designed earlier. This means having actual conversations with real people, not just intending to reach out when you need help.

Tell someone about your 28-day implementation plan. Ask for their support in specific ways. Set up your first accountability check-in. Make this support real and active, not theoretical.

The Obstacle Preparation

Review the obstacles you identified and the strategies you developed. Which obstacles are most likely to appear in your first 28 days? Make sure your prevention and response strategies are ready to implement, not just written down.

This isn't pessimistic thinking - it's realistic preparation that increases your chances of working through challenges successfully.

The Success Measurement Setup

Implement the measurement system you designed. Set up whatever tracking method you chose. Schedule your weekly and monthly assessments. Make measurement as easy and automatic as possible.

Remember, the goal of measurement is to help you see progress and learn from experience, not to create additional pressure or busy work.

The Momentum Plan

Define how you'll maintain momentum when motivation inevitably decreases. What will you do during weeks when you don't feel like engaging with your change work? How will you reconnect with your deeper reasons for transformation?

Having a plan for low-motivation periods before they occur dramatically increases your chances of working through them successfully.

The Integration Attention

Decide how you'll pay attention to the ripple effects of your focused change. What will you watch for in other areas of your life? How will you consciously connect progress in your focus area to improvements elsewhere?

This attention to integration is what transforms focused change into whole-life transformation.

The Starting Decision

Finally, decide exactly when you'll begin. Not "soon" or "next week" but the specific day and time you'll take your first intentional action.

Transformation begins with a specific decision at a specific moment. Make that decision now.

The Implementation Commitment

Your journey from insight to transformation begins tomorrow. You have everything you need: clear identity, compelling vision, honest assessment, strategic priorities, detailed plans, support systems, and measurement methods.

What you do in the next 28 days will determine whether this book becomes another interesting read or the beginning of the integrated life you've envisioned.

The planning phase is complete. The implementation phase begins now.

You know who you are. You know what you want to build. You know how to get there.

Now go build it.

TWENTY-NINE

Day 28: The Daily Choice

Yesterday's home runs don't win today's games

Twenty-eight days ago, you started this journey because you were tired of living a fragmented life. You had success but lacked authenticity. You had achievements but struggled with integration.

Over these four weeks, you've done the deep work: discovered your authentic identity, cast a compelling vision, assessed your reality honestly, and created strategic plans for transformation.

But here's what you need to understand as this structured phase ends: all the insights you've gained, all the clarity you've achieved, all the plans you've made - none of it guarantees what happens tomorrow.

Yesterday's home runs don't win today's games. And yesterday's breakthroughs don't create today's authenticity.

***

The Daily Reset Reality

Every morning, you wake up with the same choice: Will you live from your authentic identity today, or will you slip back into the fragmented patterns that feel familiar and safe?

This choice doesn't get easier just because you've spent 28 days thinking about it. In fact, it often gets harder because now you're aware of the gap between who you want to be and who you default to being under pressure.

The person you were yesterday - even if yesterday was your most authentic, integrated day ever - is not automatically the person you'll be today. Authenticity isn't a achievement you unlock once and keep forever. It's a daily decision you have to make over and over again.

***

The Momentum Illusion

Right now, you probably feel momentum from the work you've done. You have clarity about your identity, excitement about your vision, and confidence in your plan. This momentum feels powerful, and it is - for now.

But momentum is temporary. The insights that feel life-changing today will feel routine in two weeks. The commitment that feels unshakeable right now will waver when life gets complicated. The clarity you have about your authentic self will get foggy when you're under stress.

This isn't a character flaw or a sign that you haven't done the work well enough. This is the normal cycle of growth. Breakthrough, integration, plateau, challenge, choice, breakthrough again.

Successful people don't avoid this cycle - they expect it and prepare for it.

**

The Fresh Start Trap

There's a dangerous moment that comes after intensive self-discovery work like you've just completed. You feel like a new person with new insights and new possibilities. You want to live differently starting right now.

This fresh start feeling is motivating, but it's also dangerous because it can make you think that change should feel easy now that you "know better."

The truth is that knowing what to do and consistently doing it are completely different challenges. Your old patterns didn't disappear just because you gained new awareness of them. Your default responses didn't change just because you identified better alternatives.

Real transformation happens when you choose your new patterns repeatedly, especially when you don't feel like it, especially when the old patterns feel easier, especially when no one would notice if you took the convenient path.

***

The Practice Mindset

The most successful people at lasting change don't think of authenticity as something they achieve - they think of it as something they practice.

Like a musician who never stops practicing scales, or an athlete who never stops working on fundamentals, integrated people never stop practicing the basics of authentic living.

They practice showing up as themselves when it's uncomfortable. They practice making decisions from their values when it's inconvenient. They practice having difficult conversations when they'd rather avoid conflict. They practice setting boundaries when saying yes would be easier.

This practice mindset removes the pressure of perfection and creates space for the repetition that builds lasting change.

***

The Compound Daily Choice

Every day from now on, you'll face dozens of small choices between authenticity and performance, between integration and fragmentation, between showing up fully or giving people whatever version seems most convenient.

Choose to answer honestly when someone asks how you're doing, rather than giving the expected "fine."

Choose to speak up about something that matters to you, rather than staying quiet to avoid waves.

Choose to be present during family time, rather than mentally reviewing your work to-do list.

Choose to act from your values in a challenging situation, rather than doing whatever feels expedient.

These choices seem small in the moment, but they compound over time into the life you actually live. Each authentic choice makes the next authentic choice slightly easier. Each integrated decision strengthens your capacity for integration.

***

The Long Game Strategy

The work you've done over these 28 days has prepared you to play the long game of authentic living. You now have the tools, the awareness, and the strategy to make good choices consistently over time.

But playing the long game requires patience with yourself and commitment to the process rather than attachment to perfect outcomes.

Some days you'll choose authenticity and it will feel natural and rewarding. Some days you'll choose authenticity and it will feel difficult and costly. Some days you'll slip back into old patterns and have to recommit to your authentic path.

All of these experiences are normal parts of the long game. Success isn't measured by never falling back into old patterns - it's measured by how quickly you recognize when you've drifted and how readily you choose to recommit to your authentic path.

***

The Daily Renewal Practice

Because authenticity is a daily choice rather than a permanent achievement, you need daily practices that reconnect you with your authentic identity and recommit you to integrated living.

This might be a morning routine that reminds you who you are and what you're building. This might be an evening reflection that celebrates authentic choices and learns from inauthentic ones. This might be weekly planning that aligns your schedule with your values. This might be monthly reviews that assess your integration and make necessary adjustments.

The specific practices matter less than the consistent attention to who you're being and whether it aligns with who you want to be.

***

Your Daily Challenge: The Commitment to Daily Choice

Today, instead of completing another exercise, you're making a commitment to the ongoing work of daily authentic choice.

The Daily Choice Commitment

Recognize that every day from now on, you'll wake up and have to choose again between authenticity and performance, between integration and fragmentation, between showing up as yourself or as whoever seems most convenient for the situation.

This choice doesn't get easier just because you've done this work. If anything, it gets more conscious, which means you're more aware of when you're choosing convenience over authenticity.

The Practice Pledge

Commit to approaching authenticity as a practice rather than an achievement. You're not trying to become perfectly integrated and then coast. You're committing to the ongoing practice of choosing authenticity, especially when it's difficult.

The Long Game Mindset

Embrace the long game approach to transformation. Some days will feel like breakthrough days. Some will feel like setback days. Most will feel like ordinary days where you make ordinary choices that compound into extraordinary results over time.

Your success will be measured not by perfect consistency, but by your willingness to keep choosing authenticity even after you've failed to do so.

The Daily Renewal System

Establish whatever daily or weekly practices will help you stay connected to your authentic identity and committed to integrated living. This might be as simple as asking yourself each morning "How do I want to show up today?" and each evening "How did I show up today?"

The goal isn't to create another obligation on your schedule. The goal is to maintain conscious awareness of the daily choice between authenticity and performance.

**

Tomorrow's Choice

Tomorrow morning, you'll wake up as the same person you were 28 days ago in terms of your circumstances, your relationships, and your responsibilities. The only thing that will be different is your awareness of the choice you have and your tools for making that choice consistently.

Will you choose to show up as your authentic self, or will you slip back into the comfortable patterns of performing for others?

Will you choose to integrate your values into your daily decisions, or will you compartmentalize them for when it's convenient?

Will you choose to be the same person everywhere you go, or will you fragment yourself across different contexts?

These questions will be waiting for you tomorrow. And the next day. And every day after that.

The work you've done over these 28 days has prepared you to answer them well. But the answers still require daily choice, daily commitment, and daily courage.

***

The Real Work Begins Tomorrow

Your 28 days of discovery and planning weren't the transformation - they were the preparation for transformation. The real work begins tomorrow when you start making the daily choices that turn insight into reality.

You know who you are. You know what you want to build. You know how to get there.

Tomorrow, you get to prove it to yourself through your choices.

And the next day, you get to prove it again.

This is the work of a lifetime, and it's the most important work you'll ever do.

Are you ready to choose authenticity, not just once, but again and again, day after day?

The choice is yours. And it starts tomorrow.

THIRTY

Conclusion

Four weeks ago, you picked up this book because something wasn't working. You had success, but it felt hollow. You had achievements, but they came at the cost of everything else that mattered. You were winning in some areas of life while losing in others, and the constant switching between different versions of yourself was exhausting.

You were living a half-cake life, and you knew there had to be something better.

Today, you have that something better - not as a finished product, but as a clear path forward.

***

What You've Accomplished

In 28 days, you've done work that most people never do in a lifetime. You've:

Discovered your authentic identity - You know who you are when you strip away all the roles, expectations, and performances. You have a clear "I Am" statement that captures your core essence and can guide every decision you make.

Cast a compelling vision - You've moved beyond just knowing what you don't want to creating a specific picture of the integrated life you're building. You know what it looks like when someone shows up as the same authentic person everywhere they go.

Faced reality honestly - You've looked at where you currently are without sugar-coating or making excuses. You know your gaps, your obstacles, and your starting point. This honesty is the foundation for all lasting change.

Created a strategic plan - You've chosen your ONE focus area, broken it down into achievable milestones, designed weekly action steps, built accountability systems, and prepared for obstacles. You have a roadmap, not just good intentions.

Most importantly, you've proven to yourself that integration is possible. You've seen the path from fragmentation to wholeness, and you have everything you need to walk that path consistently.

***

The Gift You're Giving

The integrated life you're building isn't just about your own satisfaction and well-being. Every time you choose authenticity over performance, you give others permission to do the same. Every time you refuse to sacrifice what matters most for what seems urgent, you model a different way of being successful.

Your children are watching how you handle the tension between external expectations and internal values. Your colleagues are noticing what it looks like when someone leads from authenticity rather than ego. Your friends are seeing what's possible when someone refuses to compartmentalize their life into competing priorities.

You're not just changing your own life - you're changing what's possible in every relationship and community you're part of.

***

The Ripple Effect

As you continue this journey, you'll discover that authentic, integrated living creates ripple effects you never expected:

Your increased presence at home will improve your family relationships in ways that surprise you.

Your alignment between values and actions will increase your confidence and decision-making ability.

Your refusal to be different people in different contexts will deepen trust and respect in all your relationships.

Your focus on what truly matters will create space for the personal growth and contribution you've always wanted to make.

Your example of integrated living will inspire others to examine their own fragmentation and consider what authentic success could look like for them.

These ripples will extend far beyond what you can see or measure, touching lives and possibilities in ways you may never fully know.

✢✢✢

The Courage You've Shown

It takes courage to look honestly at your life and admit that external success isn't enough. It takes courage to stop performing different versions of yourself for different audiences. It takes courage to prioritize authenticity over approval, presence over productivity, and integration over the scattered approach that society rewards.

You've shown that courage over these 28 days, and that same courage will carry you forward as you continue building the life you've envisioned.

***

The Long View

The work you've done here isn't a 28-day program you've completed - it's a foundation you'll build on for the rest of your life. The questions you've explored about identity, vision, reality, and strategy aren't questions you answer once and forget. They're questions you'll return to regularly as you grow and as your life evolves.

This is good news, not bad news. It means you'll never outgrow the need for conscious attention to authenticity and integration. It means there's always more depth to discover, more alignment to create, more ways to show up fully for the life you're living.

***

The Promise You Made

When you started this journey, you made an implicit promise to yourself: that you wouldn't settle for a half-cake life anymore. That you would stop giving your best energy to what matters least and your leftover energy to what matters most. That you would find a way to be successful without sacrificing your soul.

You now have everything you need to keep that promise.

You have the awareness to recognize when you're slipping into old patterns. You have the tools to realign when you notice you've drifted. You have the vision to guide your choices toward what you're building. You have the strategy to create sustainable change rather than temporary improvement.

Most importantly, you have the proven ability to do hard things and create positive change in your life.

***

The Invitation Continues

The invitation remains the same as it was on Day 1: to stop living a half-cake life and start showing up more authentically everywhere you go.

But now you know what accepting that invitation actually looks like. You know it's not about perfection or dramatic transformation overnight. It's about the daily choice to be yourself rather than perform for others. It's about the consistent commitment to let your values guide your decisions rather than letting urgency or approval-seeking drive your choices.

It's about refusing to come home to half a cake in any area of your life.

***

The Question That Changes Everything

As you move forward from here, carry this question with you:

How much of the cake are you coming home to?

Not just tonight, but in your work, your relationships, your personal growth, your contribution to the world. Are you showing up fully for the life you're living, or are you giving pieces of yourself to so many different demands that there's never enough left for what matters most?

This question will guide you when motivation fades and old patterns feel appealing. It will remind you why you started this journey and what you're building with your daily choices.

***

The Truth About You

Here's what I know to be true about you after the work you've done:

You have everything you need to live an integrated, authentic life.

You're capable of being the same confident, genuine person everywhere you go.

You can have professional success without sacrificing personal presence.

You can honor your values while achieving your goals.

You can show up fully for the life you're living instead of just surviving it.

The only question is whether you will choose to do these things consistently, especially when it's difficult, especially when the old patterns feel easier, especially when no one else would notice if you took the convenient path.

***

Your Next Chapter

As you close this book and move into your next chapter, remember that you're not alone in this work. There are others who have chosen the path of authenticity and integration, and there are others who are just beginning the journey you've been on.

Be patient with yourself as you practice what you've learned. Be gentle with yourself when you fall back into old patterns. Be proud of yourself for having the courage to build something authentic and lasting.

And remember: every day is a new opportunity to show up as yourself, to choose presence over performance, to refuse half measures in any area of your life.

You have the map. You have the tools. You have the courage.

Now go build the integrated life you've envisioned, one authentic choice at a time.

The world needs who you really are, not who you think you should be.

And you deserve to live as yourself, fully and authentically, in every area of your life.

No more half cakes. No more fragmented living. No more settling for external success at the cost of internal wholeness.

You know who you are. You know what you're building. You know how to get there.

Now go show up more.

www.ingramcontent.com/pod-product-compliance
Lightning Source LLC
Chambersburg PA
CBHW070527090426
42735CB00013B/2885